Taking Charge of My Life

Personal Essays by
Today's College Students

TOWNSEND PRESS   Marlton, NJ 08053

To All Those Who Wrote an Essay for the Scholarship Program

Ordering information:

Individuals may order *Taking Charge of My Life*
for $3.00 per book ($2.00 for the book; $1.00
for shipping costs). Send a check or money order
(payable to Townsend Press) to the address below.

Bookstores may order the book for $2.00 net plus
shipping costs.

Send orders to:

**Townsend Press, Inc.
Pavilions at Greentree—408
Marlton, NJ 08053**

Teachers who wish desk copies may write to the
above address or call our toll-free number:

1-800-772-6410

Contents

Preface

The personal essays in this collection have been written by college students from across the country in response to the topic "Taking Charge of My Life." The essays are among hundreds of papers submitted as entries in a scholarship program conducted by Townsend Press. Students had in common the fact that they had taken at least one developmental reading or writing course upon entering college.

To apply, students were asked to describe in 1,000 to 2,500 words the challenges, both internal and external, that they had to face in getting to college. A panel of editors and teachers then read the essays for both content and form—for the power of the details as well as the overall effectiveness of the writing.

Scholarships included a first-place award of $2,500, five second-place awards of $1,000, fifteen third-place awards of $500, and a select number of honorable mentions at $100. All of the first-, second-, and third-place essays are reproduced here, along with a representative number of the honorable mentions. Some essays have been lightly edited to correct typos or obvious grammatical errors. A list of all award winners and their schools appears at the back of the book.

We think you will find, as we did, that reading the essays is an extraordinary experience. The authors have put a good deal of time, thought, and feeling into their writing; they have shared much about their lives. Many of the essays reveal people who, despite enormous challenges, have taken strong, positive steps to make their lives what they want them to be.

Several themes run through the essays. One theme is that the way people treat each other matters immeasurably. That treatment can be destructive, as represented by the following two essay excerpts:

- I learned to fail as a small child. The lessons taught in my family had little to do with succeeding in school or life. I was a frail and petite girl who learned early that my ideas and perceptions were worthless. I remember a time coming home after school when I was in the fourth grade. I was wearing my brown and white checkered dress. I was the first one to arrive of the four children. My mother was sitting in the kitchen talking to a friend and sipping coffee. I set my school books on the kitchen table and greeted them. Mom turned and asked me, "Is the wall black or white?" She was pointing at our white kitchen wall. I replied, "The wall is white." She slapped my face. My cheek stung and tears filled my eyes. I looked to her friend, who stoically sat there and did nothing. At that moment, I tried to figure out what was happening. My mother then asked me again, "What color is the wall, Stacy?" Hurt and angry, I looked at her and said, "The wall is black." Mom looked at her friend and smiled. I picked up my school books and went to my room and cried. I learned in grade school that you do not challenge authority and that I was of little value.

- It was my sixth grade teacher, Mrs. Evans, that made me fear and learn to hate school. I was a shy, quiet kid that just happened to look like the class troublemaker. She mistook me for this other boy, and from then on out, branded me a troublemaker. Every day, while the other kids in my class were learning about the countries and customs of the world, she made me sit in a windowless storage room, all alone. I honestly believe that this nightmarish experience scarred me for the rest of my school years. It made me afraid of school, afraid to ask questions or to seek out help.

Or the treatment can be positive, in the form of caring advice from a friend, counselor, parent, or teacher. For example, an author who overcame a learning disabilty writes in her essay:

- I was teased, told I was stupid and that I would never amount to anything. I believed all of it and hated everything about myself. I felt that way until my junior year. It took an English teacher to help me see my self-worth. He stopped teaching long enough to become a friend. He said it didn't matter what people thought about me. He told me, "Sherry, I know that you are not stupid. Just don't listen to them. They don't really know what you are like. You have to learn that you don't have to depend on what other people say to create who you are." This helped me to see who I was regardless of what others said or thought. Now I knew differently.

And the recipient of the first-place scholarship writes in her essay:

- I had reached a point in my life where I felt I could sink no lower. It seemed I couldn't die, yet I found the thought of living life as I had been unbearable. After hearing the stories of the people in Alcoholics Anonymous, I had something that I hadn't had for a very long time. I had a glimmer of hope. A counselor told me that my life was worth living, that I had a lot to offer, and that I was capable. The first time I heard the words, "You are capable," I felt stunned; I asked her to repeat the words. I found myself standing in the hall, as this woman was telling me that I was capable, with a big question mark on my face. It was as if I had never before heard these positive kinds of things. While growing up, I heard negative messages much more than I had heard anything that soothed my soul like the words the counselor was now saying to me.

In the essays there are many such testimonials to the power of care, attention, and kindness.

Another theme in the papers is that the initial hesitation and fear about returning to school are followed by pleasure and even joy in learning. The experiences of two authors upon returning to school could speak for many:

- Finally the summer ended and school began. I dressed in jeans and a sweatshirt and slung my book bag over my shoulder and set out for my first class. The butterflies in my stomach felt like elephants marching around inside of me. I found my first class and sat down. I looked around and thought, "My God, they are just babies. I must look like a wrinkled, pathetic, old antique to them." It didn't take long for me to realize they didn't care about my age. I was just one of them, a student. As the days went on and the professors gave the assignments, I raced home and began my homework. My mind came up with ideas that amazed even me. My classmates seemed genuinely interested in the essays, and the professors acted like I had something worthwhile to contribute. I was having the time of my life.

- There are times when, in my eagerness and hunger for knowledge, that I push beyond my limited capabilities. My head feels as if my brain is swelling, and I become tired and angry with myself at the slow pace I seem to be progressing in. That is when I fight even harder against my lack of understanding with more study until exhaustion sets in and I am unable to fight anymore. On many late nights, I have heard a voice within me saying,

"Why don't you just give up? Why put yourself through this torture?" But then I visualize a baby chick trying to burst out of its egg. I can almost hear the sound it makes while chipping away at the confining encasement. I rest for a while, find a temporary outlet to take my mind off my tiring fight, and begin anew hours later. I have a brain capable of learning, but was denied the opportunity as a youth. Stupid I am not! I am merely unlearned.

Here are some other themes to be found in the essays: the importance of developmental classes in preparing students for success in college; the complex family and financial adjustments that must be made to go to school; the often destructive power of peer groups, especially in high school; the inability of many high schools to serve as a positive force in students' lives; the widespread escape from an unhappy family through drugs, alcohol, and early marriage; the need for self-honesty and self-knowledge in changing one's life; the extraordinary value of social support systems such as Alcoholics Anonymous; the capacity to endure and the persistence of dreams.

The most common theme woven throughout the essays is an inspiring one. Time and again, people experience bad luck and often great hardship that make them feel they have lost control over their lives. But almost without fail, in the midst of pain and difficulty, something happens. A spark ignites and begins to grow. In the case of one author, the spark was kindled by a poem that a counselor gave her at her high school graduation:

> Only as high as I reach can I grow;
> Only as deep as I look can I see;
> Only as much as I dream can I be.

In some cases, the spark is ignited by the thought of a loved one:

- I quickly took an inventory—foreign-born, with not a great command of the English language, no money, no job training and two kids in college. The future looked bleak.

  But it did not stop. My father died. I loved him so much, and he was always my source of strength in need. Mother became ill.

  I felt very hurt, lonely, angry, and very sorry for myself.

  I remembered a saying my Dad would quote to me when things were going wrong and the future looked black. He may have gotten this quote from the Spanish edition of *Reader's Digest*. He would say, "My dear, it is always the darkest when you are fresh out of matches."

"Dad, I am out of matches." Or so I thought.

I decided to make my life something worthwhile by helping people. I wanted to help and heal. Maybe, at the same time, heal myself.

I appeared before the college doors with my knees shaking and full of doubt. I wanted to be a nurse.

I enrolled in college. I was proud of myself for not falling into the garbage pit waiting so close by.

- As I raise the gun to my head, I look up and see an outline of a face breaking through the darkness in front of me. Impulsively, words of anger start to explode from inside of me as my mouth opens. But suddenly, the outline image becomes the face of my two-year-old son. I pause for a moment as I stare into his face and say to myself, "What am I doing?" Without words, I understand every thought as I read his facial expressions. His head is tilted to one side, and his sleepy eyes look upwards at me as he wrinkles his eyebrows curiously as if to say, "What's wrong, Daddy?" Thoughts of my death force me to realize that my relief from life would have a devastating effect on my children and wife. Trying hard to fight back the tears rolling down my face, I reach out and embrace my son. His embrace of love and almost adult-like understanding sends chills up my spine as I think how close I came to leaving my family. At that moment I found the courage and determination to face and take control of my life.

  The next morning, when my wife came home from work, I kept her up for several hours explaining my plans to go to college and get a degree.

In a number of cases, the spark emerges from within:

- At first it was enough to enjoy my children's accomplishments and to be "Mom's taxi," but my heart began speaking something else to me. Its words were terrifying, yet so challenging that I couldn't get them out of my mind. My heart's desire was telling me that I had more to do and more to give in this life, and now for the first time I had the opportunity. I felt that an education would be the only way to get on the path to a new life.

- While sitting—my most perfected art—and watching television one night, I was dreaming of all the things I would not be able to get my son for his thirteenth birthday. Thirteen, he was no longer a baby. He was turning into a teenager before my eyes. It won't be long before he becomes a young adult. Then he becomes completely independent. Next, he'll move into an apartment of his own. Oh my God! Then he will fall in love, get married, and have children! I'm going to be a lonely, old, fat grandmother facing the rest of my life with nothing to fill the void! Wake up, Ruth! Take charge of your life before it's over!

Who said that? Is it really possible that there is a little voice inside my head that can scream loud enough to register on a Richter scale? I have read about it in children's books, and I had watched it happen on television, but now it was happening to me. My inner self was wanting to come out. Most of all, my inner self was wanting to learn, to grow, and to become something.

After another week or two, I decided to check into the possibility of furthering my education.

Whatever the source, the spark grows into a determination not to settle for too little in life. And that resolve is accompanied by a belief that enrolling in college is a key to a more hopeful future.

The decision to go to college is part of a larger, often passionate commitment to the future. As one person writes at the close of his essay:

- Here I am, starting from the bottom. My educational background is next to nothing, but I won't let that get me down. I know that I'll probably have to work harder and longer than others my age, but I also know that it will be worth it. . . . Yes, there are so many paths that I have yet to travel, and so much work and hardship that I have yet to endure, but this is my dream. As I see it, we are all given two choices in life. We either choose to succeed, and overcome our obstacles, or give in and stop trying. No matter how long it takes, or how much work I have to do, I will make my dream a reality.

These remarks and ones similar to them appear in essay after essay. They speak eloquently not only of enormous challenges but of people rising to those challenges. The essays in this book, and the hundreds of deserving essays for which there was neither an award nor space in this book, have been written by extraordinary people.

The Editors

Ricki Gutierrez

I had been drunk and high for the better part of nine months. I was living in an ex-lover's apartment while he was paying the bills and waiting for me to get it together and get a job. He was on the verge of throwing me out. I had been doing things for a long time that were against my moral values, hanging out with people with whom I said I would never hang out. I was doing things for money I said I would never do. I was forty pounds overweight, thirty-two years old, and a high school dropout. I felt hopeless—completely and thoroughly hopeless. I had been out the night before with an ex-con drinking and carrying on.

I felt so much shame because of my behavior that I could not hold my head up. I thought of my son who had lived with his father since age three; he was now fourteen. I felt more guilt than I could stand about all the times I had stood him up, for all the times I lied to him, been late to pick him up, and neglected him when he was with me. I thought of the few friends I had left that were fed up with me because they never knew what I was going to do anymore. I felt alone and worthless.

I was drinking rum that night, straight shots of rum. I sat alone in the apartment and drew the conclusion that the world would be a much better place if I were not here. I believed this with all my heart, so I went across the breezeway where Jerry (my ex) was staying, at his mother's apartment. I took a full bottle of an anti-depressant that had been prescribed for his mother, without anyone noticing. I went back to the unkempt apartment I was existing in. Then, I went to the phone to call a friend that was supposed to have come over for spaghetti, but had stood me up. I took another shot of rum while I talked to my friend. I counted out fifty pills in one pile and fifty in another. Then, I scooped up the first pile of pills, crammed them in my mouth, took the glass of water off the table, and began to swallow. I then said good-bye to my friend. I said I would talk to her later, not letting on for a minute what I

1

was doing. I hung up the phone and swallowed the second fifty pills. After that, I walked over to the sofa to lie down and die.

Some hours later, when I came to in intensive care, I felt so disgusted, disappointed, ashamed, and angry. I wanted to run or disappear. "Why the hell am I still here?!" my mind screamed. I spent five days in intensive care before being escorted by the police to the Crisis Center, a detoxification center in the city where I lived. I felt as if I were walking around dead, not only because it's so hard to come off drugs and alcohol, but because I was carrying around the weight of my entire life. I left after seven days, again ushered by the police, but this time to the state hospital. I was so afraid, for the state mental hospital is where I always feared I belonged. And I was nothing less than terrified of being locked up in a "nut ward."

Instead of the mental hospital, I was sent to the neighboring drug and alcohol treatment center. This is where I was to begin the long and slow road to recovery, back to myself. I was told while I was there that I had a disease called alcoholism and that I was not a bad person, in spite of what I had always believed. I heard the stories of the courageous people that come to the treatment center from Alcoholics Anonymous. They said they had made some of the same or similar choices in life that I had made. They had been involved in destructive relationships such as I had been: divorces, DUI's, and the list goes on. Nevertheless, they were making changes in their lives. They said I could too.

I had reached a point in my life where I felt I could sink no lower. It seemed I couldn't die, yet I found the thought of living life as I had been unbearable. After hearing the stories of the people in Alcoholics Anonymous, I had something that I hadn't had for a very long time. I had a glimmer of hope. A counselor told me that my life was worth living, that I had a lot to offer, and that I was capable. The first time I heard the words, "You are capable," I felt stunned; I asked her to repeat the words. I found myself standing in the hall, as this woman was telling me that I was capable, with a big question mark on my face. It was as if I had never before heard these positive kinds of things. While growing up, I heard negative messages much more than I had heard anything that soothed my soul like the words the counselor was now saying to me.

In the thirty-one days that I was in the treatment center, I began a journey inward. I've been told by counselors and by my new friends that, while the journey is very painful at times, the only way out of the pain is to go back through it and face it head-on. I had denied the facts of my childhood long enough; in fact, I had almost denied the facts to my grave. When I was asked about my childhood, my response was always something of this nature: "My mother did the best she could do." I would focus on the few pleasant things and tell these things only, unless I was very drunk. And, on occasion, I would tell some of the darker things. The truth of the matter is, while my mother may have been doing the best she could do, it was by no stretch of the imagination good enough.

Before I was born, my mother had already been married three times and had three small girls besides myself. While married to her third husband, she began drinking and dancing with her husband's best friend. She became pregnant with me by this friend of her husband's. I was told this story by one of my sisters at about the age of twelve. My first memory is around the age of three. My mother led me by the hand into a baby-sitter's apartment. I felt afraid to stay with this man, and my sisters seemed afraid also. After my mother left, the man made pallets on the floor and asked us who wanted to sleep with him. For some reason I was chosen, and as we were lying there, in the still dark night, the man whispered something to me. He placed my small three-year-old hand on something soft and clammy. I felt squeamish. My hand jerked away from what it felt. The man whispered something else to me, and once again, he placed my hand there, this time squeezing my hand after he placed it where he wanted it. I knew this time not to move my hand. The man finally went to sleep; so did I.

The first of a long line of men in my mother's life that I remember was a tall, olive-complected, dark-haired man. My sisters and I were in bed; my mother was sleeping with this man in another part of the small house. I awakened the next morning to this man scolding and shaming me for wetting in the bed. I was not much older than three.

Soon after, another olive-complected, dark-haired man entered our lives. I remember his broad shoulders and dark eyes. The first time I saw him, he bent down to lift my small body from the floor. I felt his very large hands slip under my armpits as he lifted me up to his chest, holding my face at his. I felt timid and shy as I looked at him. I got the feeling that this man was going to be my daddy, and I wanted a daddy. He placed me back on the ground with as much ease as when he picked me up. He then offered me a piece of candy, and I turned to go and play alone. My sisters were no longer living with us; they were now living with their fathers. Mother married this man, whose name was Freddie, and the hope I had for a father soon turned into one of the most startling and gruesome nightmares of my life.

Freddie and my mother spent many hours in their bedroom. One time I crept to the door and peeked in at them; later my mother went to the bathroom, and Freddie came to the room where I was now playing, grabbed me by the collar, and said in a low whisper while looking straight into my eyes, "If you ever do that again, I will kill you."

I was still wetting the bed at age 4. Freddie told my mother he would "break me" of wetting the bed. One morning I awakened to Freddie yanking the cover off me. He saw that I had, indeed, wet the bed. He then pulled me violently from the bed and stuck my face in the wet circle, rubbed my nose in it as if I were a dog. He tried to "break" me in this manner often.

Next, he informed me that if I were going to act like a baby and wet the bed, I would be treated like a baby: I would have to wear a diaper the next time I wet the bed. He seemed very pleased with this new idea. I felt afraid and absolutely helpless. I was at the mercy of this man, and he had none. Although my mother was in the house while much of this was going on, she was simply not available. Why, I don't know.

The next day I was not only wearing a diaper, but I was made to parade up and down the sidewalk in front of our house so that the kids that were playing outside would see. I tried to walk softly so the children wouldn't see me. I remember well how I longed to become invisible. We moved often; therefore, I never had a chance to put down roots or get to know the neighboring children; but, at times like these, I can't say that I really wanted to get acquainted with my neighbors. I felt so ashamed, and less than human.

Freddie didn't like me around; so, often, when we had our meals, he and my mother would sit in the living room and eat together while I sat at the table alone. One night, I spilled my milk. Freddie came over to the chair where I sat, placed his hand on the back of my head, lifted me up, lowered me to my knees on the floor, pushed my head down, and said, "Lick it up."

Later when I reached school age, nothing changed except the houses we lived in and my mother's husbands. When I would have homework, my mother would send me to my room to do it. When I came out of the room to be tested by her and I didn't get it right, she would scream that she had things to do, and "What in the hell have you been doing in there anyway?" She would slap me across the face, take me by the arm and shove me back into my room. After that I would cry so hard I couldn't think. I soon quit bringing my homework home. I lied and said I didn't have any homework.

This is not an attempt to bash Freddie, my mother, or anyone else that has crossed my path over the years, but child abuse is real, and it does interfere with a person's ability to succeed in our world. These are grotesque stories, and hard to read, I'm sure. They are equally as hard for me to relive as I write; nevertheless, these are things that have shaped my opinion of and feelings for myself and the world in which I live. These are the obstacles I've had to overcome to get into college, and these are the obstacles I will have to continue crossing in order to get my degree.

I want to overcome the abuse of my childhood. I want to live, and I want the education I feel I was robbed of as a child due to physical, mental, emotional, sexual abuse and the instability of moving from place to place.

I'm taking charge of my life in these ways: I have not seen my mother in two years. I have been in therapy for three and a half years. My relationship with my son is improving, and I haven't had a drink or a drug in over two and a half years. I finished my first semester of college with the highest grades possible in effective reading, study skills, spelling, and College Writing II.

If I win this scholarship, I will use the money to continue my education. I want to be a part of the mainstream of life, to be able to take care of myself, pay my bills, take vacations, enjoy life, and contribute to society in a positive way.

Bettie Jo Mellott

Meg sat in a wheelchair in the cafeteria at the Columbus Rehabilitation Center. With her useless limbs and facial scars, she looked like a cerebral palsy patient, not like the victim of an industrial injury. Actually, she had been raped, beaten, and left for dead by a prisoner at the correctional facility where she had been a medication nurse. Her body was permanently damaged, but her soul and spirit were on fire for life. Determination and gusto, it just radiated from everywhere, her eyes, her smile, and even the proud, upright way she sat in her wheelchair. I was immediately drawn to her. What an inspiration she became to me! We shared many similarities, but the greatest difference was that I improved and went home. She's still there. I felt so ashamed of my own fears and shortcomings regarding my injuries. My name is Bettie Jo (B.J.) Mellott. I am 43 years old, a mother, and a full-time sophomore at Ohio University Eastern in St. Clairsville, Ohio.

At the time I met Meg in the rehabilitation center, I had encountered severe trauma in my own life, not only physically, as my body was now damaged, but my emotional psyche was in a fragile state. It happened in January of 1989. I was severely injured as an L.P.N. in the CCU due to a lifting accident. The memories are vague and sketchy, but I do remember many days of lying in the hospital, pain coursing through my body. The worst feeling, however, was the sense of helplessness. When I got to go home, I was on weeks of bed rest followed by months of physical therapy, more treatments, tests, and several more hospitalizations. I had to use a walker to even be up for only minutes a day, then half-hours, then one, two, three hours, etc. I had problems with my balance, trying to use my legs. I was so weak physically and emotionally. Some days I didn't even want to try. I was so discouraged, having to face the reality that maybe I'd never be well, trying to make adjustments to the way my life was now.

My family was also struggling with me. My husband Herman, who drives a school bus full time, now found himself in the role of both mother and father, trying to keep up with everything. That meant milking 38 cows twice a day, seven days a week, keeping up with a large garden, cooking, cleaning, taking care of our two sons Mikel and Mark, who were eight and 16 at the time. I could only come home on weekends and still wasn't much help to him. He was brave, but becoming exhausted with all the stress and hard work. My heart broke for him every time I saw his haggard face and tired body. The thought crossed my mind many times that he would want to chuck it all and just walk out or ask me to leave, but it never came to that. He stuck by me through it all, and I thank God for his dedication and unending love. The hardest part was knowing that I couldn't change things no matter how much I wanted to make them better. I kept hoping I'd get off the crutches I was using and would be whole again.

There was much that I couldn't change, but I was still determined to take charge of my life. In September of 1991, after much soul searching for the courage to try, I signed up for a course at Ohio University Eastern, our local college, a Credit for Life Experiences class. I was very much afraid. My self-esteem was low. Up until this time, I had not been allowed to drive over ten miles at any one time, but just getting to college one way was nearly 32 miles and practically an hour's drive. Fortunately, this university has handicapped-parking facilities and an elevator in the building, so I could get to the classes I needed. I made four trips to the class, then had to finish the rest by mail, as I had to go back to the rehab center in Columbus for another three weeks.

During this stay, I agreed to an epidural nerve block. To my dismay, I had an extreme reaction to the cortisone injected into my spinal column, which put me in the Ohio State University Hospital with a partial loss of vision in one eye for about three weeks and a temporary loss of the use of my right leg and hand. Needless to say, that set me back both physically and emotionally.

Upon release from the hospital, I decided that I wanted to attend college full time this time for real (the initial class consisted of a teacher and four students). Now it would mean dealing with the "handicap" stigma. I walked using Canadian Crutches with an odd gait which drew attention to myself. I had also gained over 60 pounds since my injury, and I felt extremely fat and ugly. I was 42 years old, and almost all the other students seemed to be 18 and beautiful. I worried myself sick over everything imaginable. After much pleading with my neurosurgeon, he tentatively released me to attend full time. I also had to prove to Worker's Compensation that I could withstand the academic and physical demands, and show my family that I wasn't hurting myself with undue stress and all the physical demands necessary to attend two or three days a week, carrying a full-time load.

I withdrew all the money I had in my savings account, paid for my tuition and books, and began winter quarter, scared to death I'd fail or flunk out, so much was riding on this trial period. In hindsight, I think all the negatives stacked against me were actually the incentives that made me that much more determined to try and prove to everyone and myself that I could succeed.

Somehow I made it through the winter quarter. It ended with my making an A, a B+, and two C+'s for 13 credit hours. I then signed up for the spring quarter and held my breath. After the Bureau of Worker's Compensation and the Doctor of Record evaluated me both physically and academically, I was allowed to continue. I even received assistance for tuition and supplies from the Bureau of Vocational Rehabilitation. I began spring quarter full of enthusiasm, determined to make better grades, take more classes, and complete as many courses as possible to be able to graduate in three years rather than four. I was so encouraged by my success and so motivated to learn more that I decided to take summer classes. I attended full time, took 21 credit hours and made the Dean's List with a 3.750 G.P.A.

All was not easy, however. I had run into my first academic obstacle: English Composition. I never had a problem verbalizing my thoughts, but apparently I had major shortcomings when it came to writing down those same thoughts. I made mistakes including comma splices, fragments, idea disorganization, and, in general, had forgotten many ground rules of semantics. Fortunately, my professor, Mr. Patrick Wood, was more than willing to help me overcome these drawbacks and academic difficulties. One of his recommendations was that I take a developmental course in writing, English 150, where the basics are re-emphasized and can be internalized more readily through repetitious lesson plans.

My many problems and the course Freshman Comp 151 ended with my getting an incomplete. Thus, in fall quarter, I did indeed take the developmental English course. Through sheer perseverance and skillful guidance of the professor, I learned how to write full sentences, spell words more accurately, punctuate a little more properly, and organize my thoughts in a more functional way. At the end of the course, I made an A- grade. I still made mistakes, as you have probably observed, but this was a major victory for me. I now had confidence.

Beginning in January (winter quarter), I will use this confidence to re-take English 151, knowing that I am much better prepared to internalize writing concepts and become a better writer.

In many ways, having an academic problem has made me appreciate the educational process even more. I learned a long time ago that life often involves struggle, but I am not a quitter. I have known much pain in life. For instance, I was engaged twice to military men who were killed while in Vietnam. I lost my home to a fire and had to start completely over. My father was killed in an auto accident, and now this injury. I feel my faith has been tested repeatedly, yet I have risen to the occasion spiritually stronger. Therefore, attending college and overcoming academic obstacles is just one more stepping stone on the pathway to my future.

Fall quarter has just ended. I carried 23 credit hours, including one nursing class at a nearby technical school. (If a student at Ohio University Eastern attends full time, he can take one free course each semester at the technical school, which I did.) The course, Community Nursing Practices, is a requirement for an Associate Degree R.N. Program. I am trying also to meet the academic requirements to sit for state boards for my R.N. license. My ultimate goal is to teach preventative health care in the Public Health Care System, or in some capacity in the high school or college level. I am also taking the appropriate classes to sit for the exam of Licensed Social Worker.

My goals are high, and the road ahead is not an easy one, but I am a survivor. In a paradoxical kind of way, I know that I am gifted. I value living. I value giving. Each day is a struggle, but I want to make a difference in the lives of other Megs and Bettie Jo's who might give up because of their pain. I am thankful for the opportunity to learn, and I plan to make the most of it. My primary goals are threefold: to be a good mother and wife, to complete the college process, and to eventually become a licensed social worker.

My family and close friends have been very supportive of me, and we have been able to apply some of these same principles in other ways in our family life. My son Mikel, now 12 years old, has recently take on the responsibility of providing a foster home and care for a Pilot Dog puppy. His name is Harris, an eight-week-old golden retriever puppy. We shall keep him until he is 13 months old. Then, he will return to the Pilot Dog, Inc. School, where he will undergo training to be a guide dog for a blind person. My son will be learning many valuable lessons through this experience that may ultimately make him a better human being.

As for myself, I still have over half of my education to complete. At present, I am registered for winter quarter. I will be taking 27 credit hours to continue with my goal of graduating in three years. Yes, I will continue to pursue my dreams. I have taken charge of my life!

There are many things beyond my control, but I have learned that taking charge means a daily deciding to enter life more fully. Life is full of obstacles, but it also is full of opportunities. It means trying, sometimes a lot of trying (e.g. this paper has involved some five rewrites). It also means the pursuit of dreams.

Ohio University Eastern will be beginning a Master's Degree for Rehabilitation Counselors program in June of 1994. Priority is being given to females, those with disabilities, and also those who reside in an Appalachian region. I meet all of those. I have spoken via telephone to the contact person in charge of this pilot program, Dr. Lisa Lopez-Lever. I feel confident that I at least have a chance at this opportunity. It is opportunities like your Scholarship Program for Developmental Reading and Writing Students that may also play an important part in my future or the future of others who are just like me, trying very hard to get an education and help themselves and others along life's journey.

Elda Sara Morgan

There have been many personal obstacles, both internal and external, in my life that I have overcome to be in college. Like others I have many challenges ahead which I'm positive I'll meet head on.

Through no fault of my own, I developed epilepsy after having German measles as a child. In grade school I was very sick and shunned by teachers who were afraid of me. These teachers had no experience or knowledge of how to treat epileptics or those with other diseases or disabilities. In my case, if I didn't understand what they were teaching, they would pass me into the next class to get rid of me. This was very difficult as I had to learn some of the things I missed in my later years.

In late elementary and junior high, my fellow classmates as well as the teachers ostracized me. During this period of time, I was pushed down the school stairs and beaten up daily. It was the loneliest period of my life, and I turned to reading and writing poetry for solace.

It wasn't until I was a sophomore in high school and a teacher saw potential in a frightened, alienated student that I began to like school. Mr. Thomas Fisher saw that I excelled in science courses and asked me to tutor fellow classmates in advanced biology. He told me because of my tutoring, one student in particular passed her entrance boards to nursing school. It was the first compliment any teacher gave me. Under his guidance, I taught a variety of science courses at Elmira Free Academy. These included genetics, cytology and cytogenetics, and ecology, while maintaining a dean's list average in all other subjects. I was the first high school student to ever teach classes in our school district. In my senior year I assisted another teacher in comparative dissection class. While a sophomore, I audited a college level course offered at Elmira Free Academy, advanced biology, but was unable to get college credit for it. This was because it was designed only for seniors to take for college credit, not sophomores.

During this same time, I wanted to be either a science teacher or nurse. My guidance counselor informed me epileptics couldn't teach or be a nurse. He told me it was better for us to be secretaries, the reason being if you were a teacher or nurse and had a seizure and something happened to the children, you could be sued. I did attempt to get into two local schools of nursing and was denied because I was an epileptic in the later part of my senior year. Also, I had a very difficult time taking hard courses because this guidance counselor insinuated I wasn't smart enough. I did take whatever class I wanted by going over his head.

It must also be noted that because of people like this guidance counselor, I was determined to prove them all wrong. I easily achieved this goal when I graduated with 28¾ credits and on the honor roll, when all that's required is 18 credits to graduate. When I received my final report card, I made an appointment to see this man and showed him my grades. I asked him never to forget you're as disabled as you want to be and as you can see, I'm not. I'm as smart as anyone else; and I walked away.

After graduation, I was referred to the New York State Office of Vocational Rehabilitation for financial assistance and training specifically suited for an epileptic. It was here that I was sent to Elmira Business Institute (EBI) as a medical secretary. When I enrolled at EBI, I told the director I didn't want anyone except my instructors to know I was an epileptic. I wanted an opportunity to be considered "normal." I was treated fairly until an instructor in my medical terminology class asked me what it was like being an epileptic in front of the class. Friends no longer spoke or had lunch with me. I was alienated due to fear. I was in a bus accident and suffered a concussion, pulled back muscles and a whiplash and never missed a day of class. When a male teacher made a pass at me two weeks before graduation, I was devastated. I finished EBI and lacked 3/10 of a point from graduating. I never went back because I hated what I was doing and how I was treated.

I had miscellaneous jobs that had no benefits or future. Most of these consisted of positions in food service. One of these employers mixed two different undiluted chemicals together, ignoring warning labels. This caused me to become severely allergic to chemicals and pesticides. This is a well-documented and frustrating disability because avoidance of these chemicals is the only way of preventing a severe allergic reaction.

After I developed this allergic reaction, I was unable to find work and ended up on public assistance. I then began attending college and, for health reasons, I had to withdraw from most of my classes in the spring and drop all of my summer classes. I completed my fall semester without any problems. During this time, I was harassed by public assistance because I was going to college. An opportunity presented itself to get off public assistance, and I left New York and moved to Colorado for 1½ years.

I then moved back to New York and found kitchen work at first. I was employed briefly as a receptionist and caseworker/pre-trial interviewer. When I lost this job, I became frustrated because the only jobs available were for restaurant work. Due to my allergy to chemicals, I was unable to work in these positions because of the sanitation requirements.

I personally began to think of any jobs I would like to do that would not further jeopardize my health. During this time, I consulted with my neurologist, who told me I was no longer considered an epileptic and didn't need medication and told me to pursue my dreams to the fullest. After seeing him, I decided on enrolling in college and pursuing my dream of being a special education teacher.

I then was employed full-time as a telemarketer/statistician for a major mail order company in Elmira. I was laid off from work in April and have worked only four weeks so far this year. Recently I spoke with the personnel director who informed me it was unlikely I'd be called back due to the lack of orders so far.

In 1990 I returned to CCC and worked my way through college until I was laid off. Balancing working 40 to 60 hours a week while attending college was difficult, but my determination on maintaining good scholastic grades was realized. When I was named to the Dean's List during this period, I was ecstatic and proud, for I knew how difficult it was and how hard I had to work for it. I am currently carrying a GPA of 3.377, and I will complete my Associate's Degree in the spring of 1993.

Presently I'm being evaluated by a physician for severe joint pain and motor difficulty in my hands. I have learned compensatory techniques that have enabled me to maintain a high grade point average so far. I am presently taping all of my lectures and using a triangular grip that helps me hold my pencil or pen.

My immediate goal is to graduate from Corning Community College and hopefully enroll in American International College in the fall of 1993.

I began my college career by taking Developmental English (EN 95) and Sentence Building (WS 103). I am currently taking Punctuation Review (WS 91) and plan on enrolling in Grammar Review (WS 92) next spring. I am taking these courses now because I am having difficulty with maintaining correct punctuation and grammar in my writing.

I'm presently looking for financial help to purchase a computer to help me do my homework and take notes. This will help me as I have great difficulty in holding a pen or pencil when writing. Currently I have mobility in my fingers, but lack the strength to hold anything for long periods of time.

I have severe financial difficulties because I am unemployed and have a severely limited area in which I can work in this area. I have approximately 18 weeks in which I can continue to receive college unemployment, and as I mentioned before have only worked four weeks this entire year. Because of this and the simple truth my parents are unable to help me out financially, I would greatly appreciate being considered for any scholarships available. If chosen, I intend to work harder than I ever have to maintain excellent grades. I am determined to get my college degree and teach those who are less fortunate than myself.

I am a hard worker who goes beyond what's expected of me. I have a deep desire to be a special education teacher. By overcoming my own personal obstacles, I feel I have a unique understanding of the importance of this position. I am not afraid of children with handicaps or disabilities. Please give me this opportunity to achieve my dream.

Christina J. Jones

"To everything, turn, turn, turn, . . . there is a season, turn, turn, turn, . . . and a time to every purpose under heaven." This verse, from a song by the Byrds, sums up the reasons for the events in my life. I am the product of a dysfunctional family and married an abusive alcoholic at the age of sixteen. My husband forbade me to finish my education, kept me a prisoner in my own home for ten years, fathered our two children, and then left me for another woman.

I am currently a single, disabled mother of two, a recovering alcoholic/addict, a felon just recently off parole, and a college student. Attending college has been a dream of mine since I was a child. Now, thanks to God, my dream has become my reality. Since my first horrifying day in the classroom, I have grown in more ways than are imaginable. I feel as though I've beaten the odds against me and am finally on my way to a productive role in society. Now, after half my life is over, I know what I want to do with my life, what I have to do to achieve it, and I am damned determined to reach my goals! My only regrets are that I didn't realize what I wanted earlier and that there is so little time left for me to use what I'm learning. Perhaps my life would have turned out differently, had my beginning been less of an obstacle.

My parents married at the tender age of sixteen. Shortly after their union, I was born. Still children themselves, they were catapulted into adult roles with adult responsibilities. Unable to face their new obligations, they divorced. At six months old I was given to my paternal grandparents to raise.

My mother didn't have much time for me. She was busy living out her life in the fast lane. I tried living with her for a while when I was eleven. But her lifestyle conflicted with the morals my grandparents instilled in me. I began to blame myself for her behavior. Thus, I became a very confused child. When circumstances became too traumatic for me, I moved back in with my grandparents. Through the years she became an alcoholic and a drug addict, and her disease took precedence over her family.

My father remarried. I tried living with him and his new family several times. I felt the need to be a part of his life. But his wife hated the sight of me and made my life a living hell. My father wasn't home much of the time. He was either working multiple jobs or out womanizing. I became the outlet of my stepmother's frustration. She was physically and mentally abusive when we were left alone. Fearing for my life and my sanity, I retreated to the home of my grandparents.

This crazy cycle repeated itself many times throughout my childhood. From Grandma's to Dad's, to Grandma's to Mom's, to Grandma's to Dad's, etc. . . . Each time I thought, "This time it will be different." I never felt like I belonged anywhere.

School was a nightmare! I changed schools three times in one year! I was an introvert as a child. I had severe emotional problems that were apparent in my grades, my attitude, and my behavior. For a number of years I thought I was retarded. I was a loner, and whenever anyone was nice to me, I'd usually cry and run off. I was so concerned about my family problems and what was wrong with me that I couldn't concentrate on anything. I usually did well enough to pass into the next grade, although most of the time promotion was by the skin of my teeth.

When I reached high school, my grades improved somewhat. I passed with at least a "C" average. I think I finally learned how to tune out most of my family problems while I was at school. I did manage to make a few friends, although I was never popular. I began to live a double life. I was one person at home and another at school. I became a people pleaser. I became who I had to be at any particular time to avoid friction. I no longer had an identity. I lost who I was.

My grandparents raised me most of my life. They loved me. I know this because of the morals and values they tried to teach me. I was the center of their world. They made me feel loved. But I still never felt like I quite belonged with them either. I remained with my grandparents until I was sixteen.

My grandparents tried to protect me from everything. So, when they found out I had a boyfriend, they sent me to the country. They figured if they could get me out of the sinful city into the solace of the country, I'd be safe.

When I got to Arkansas, I found a job as a waitress. My father had bought me an old car for my sixteenth birthday, so I did have some independence. At least I didn't have to depend on anyone to get me back and forth to work! The restaurant was a small business owned by two lovely old people. I couldn't wait to get to work each day. The three of us had such a good time. They seemed to enjoy teaching me the business as much as I enjoyed learning it. I was a waitress, cashier, dishwasher, and part-time cook. I loved working there! I felt good about myself for the first time in a long time. In the middle of the second month that I worked there, the Mrs. took ill. Mr. had to take care of her, so both of them could no longer work. To keep from closing their little business, they hired a cook and her daughter to help me run the place.

With all the ongoing pressure from my grandparents, the responsibilities of my new job, and the concern over my employers, I began to drink. At first it was a beer after work; then it was two, three, four. It seemed to relax me, help me sleep, and help me escape my problems. Nobody knew of my secret, and that's the way I wanted it.

One night after work, the people who were hired to help me in the restaurant asked me if I'd like to go for a midnight swim. It sounded delightful! The summer air was warm and the sky was lit by thousands of twinkling diamonds. It sounded so relaxing. When our shift was over, we put the top down on the car and eagerly took off to the lake. That night I met and fell in love with the man who would soon become my husband.

Randy was so different than any other boy I'd known. He was jealous, attentive, warm, loving, and naive in a cute kind of way. He put me on a pedestal. He worshipped the ground I walked on. And the most important thing of all, he told me he loved me. We fell in love and we were married two months later.

At first our marriage was everything I'd ever hoped it could be. Then he started drinking and staying out all night with the boys. I waited by the window night after night for the sound of his car and the sight of his headlights to reach the driveway. All the while I worried about his safety, wondering where he'd been, and blaming myself for his behavior. His drinking became worse; then came the beatings. What was I doing wrong? I couldn't figure it out. Maybe he'd change if I was a better wife . . . maybe if I kept house better or showed him more love. Even doing these things didn't help.

Our first child came the second year of our marriage. She was a godsend to me. Since my husband wasn't around much, I devoted my life to her. She was mine, and she loved me no matter who I was. My husband's drinking got worse and the beatings more severe. I tried everything to avoid the fights, but they came anyway. I still blamed myself for them. When our daughter was six years old, I got pregnant with our son. I took my last beating from my husband when I was four months pregnant. He came home drunk, said the child I was carrying was not his, and started hitting me in the stomach. Rage filled my heart! The next thing I knew, the tables were turned, and it was his blood that ran, not mine.

My son was born a healthy child, who happened to look just like his father. My husband's attitude changed; for about a year he tried to be a good husband and father. Then his drinking took hold of him again, and when I found out he'd fathered another child by another woman and that she was due soon, our marriage ended.

The divorce signified another of my failings. How I'd loved that man. I gave him ten years of my life. How could he have betrayed me so? Now I was faced with raising two children on my own. I didn't have enough of an education to get a job above minimum wage. My husband refused to pay child support. He hoped that in desperation I would take him back. But for the first time in my life my pride took over and refused him.

I took three jobs to support us. Although I met the bills, I didn't have much time to spend with my children. We lived this way for two years. Then one night at work, I injured my spine. I was in and out of the hospital for the next five years for weeks and months at a time. When I was home, I was limited to the activities I could perform. I had to depend on my little girl, family members, and a handful of friends to take care of me, my son, and the house. Again, I felt like a failure.

The doctor I was going to prescribed unlawful amounts of drugs for me. But I took them with no question. After all, he was a doctor; the head of rehabilitation at a major hospital surely knew what he was doing! It did relieve the pain so I could function better, so it must be the right thing to do.

Soon I was addicted to narcotics. I didn't realize it for a long time because of the rationalizations. I couldn't imagine dealing with the pain without them.

After about the third year of my addiction, I called a treatment center for help. The looks I got from my children when I reached for the pill bottle, the mood swings I went through, and the dread of facing one more day of living on drugs was more than I could stand. I needed help! They came and got me at three in the morning. I remember taking a handful of pills before they got there, thinking to myself, "Well, if I live through this, it will be the last drug I'll ever be able to take. If I don't, then I don't have to worry about it."

I woke up that next morning wondering where in the hell I was. Then I remembered what I'd done. I was mad at myself for waking up that morning. I'd really wanted to die. I spent nine days in detoxification; then I was made to participate in classes.

The center taught me about my disease and what to do to stay clean. They introduced me to a twelve-step program to help me live. But I received most of my help from a psychologist. She made me look at myself, which was horrifying! I didn't really know who I was. I had lived so many lies all of my life that I lost "me" somewhere along the line. Making that phone call was the best thing I'd ever done for myself and the most challenging. I was twenty-nine years old and didn't know how to live life on life's terms. I had absolutely no self-esteem and felt no self-worth. In my eyes I was a worthless human being with no purpose. I simply didn't deserve to live.

I worked the twelve-step program for four years. Then I quit going to meetings. I guess I thought I had it beat. That was the first mistake of many to come.

One day while outside in the garden, I fell. I was once again faced with severe pain. This scared me because I wanted to take something for it, and I knew I couldn't have narcotics. I lay in bed for three days. A friend of mine heard of my problem and came over to offer his help. I asked him to find me a joint (marijuana cigarette) to ease the pain. So he did, and that started me on pot. I abused that too. I began smoking for the feeling it gave me, not just when I was in pain. Before I knew what hit me, I was using it every day. Marijuana is an expensive drug, more than I could afford. So I would buy a small bag of it and then sell part of it so mine wouldn't cost me anything. One night I sold some to a girl who happened to be a confidential informant, and then I got busted. I went to court and was sentenced to six years in the penitentiary. I was sentenced in October, but because of the overcrowding, I didn't go down until December 27th of that same year. At least I got to spend the holidays with my children. The hardest part was saying good-by, not knowing when I'd see them again.

I had put myself through a treatment center the July before sentencing and had managed to stay clean. So I entered the women's unit drug-free. It was the most horrible experience! A person is nothing in there; a person has no rights, no freedom, and no life. It was horrible, but it opened my eyes. It was as if God said to me, "Christina, do something with the rest of your life, or you will live it out here."

I spent the days planning my future. I was determined to change no matter what it took. I didn't want to live the rest of my life on a paltry sum from the government. Spinal disease or not, I knew I could get an education and use my mind to make my way. To hell with the physical pain; I could handle it. Feeling good about myself was more important!

The day I was released it felt like God was giving me one more chance to make something of myself. That week I checked into college. I must admit I was scared to death. I had been out of school for twenty years. I didn't know if I was smart enough to make it.

Well, I am currently a student at A.S.U. with a 3.7 GPA. I will have three years clean and sober in July this year; I attend twelve-step meetings on a regular basis and help out at the local treatment facility. I've gained the love and respect of my family and friends and have a good man in my life. Attending college has given me something that I've never had before: self-esteem, self-respect, and the courage to go on. I thank God that I found it. I thank God that I'm alive.

I still suffer from chronic pain, but I have learned to deal with it. I've been recently diagnosed with a new muscle and joint disorder, but I'm not going to quit. I am determined to achieve my dream no matter what it takes.

I have learned that I am only responsible for my own behavior, that the only people I have to please are God and myself, and that nothing is impossible. I believe that everything happens for a reason, and that for every painful experience a person endures, that person is rewarded ten times with something joyful.

I hope to use my education to help other people who have walked in my shoes. There are no hopeless people, just people with no hope.

Vickie Jean Burress

The challenges in my life have been nothing but average when they are compared to other people's. I graduated from Mooresville High School in May of 1967. I did not prepare for college even though it was a secret desire of mine. I only wanted to graduate and dive right into the big wonderful world that awaited me. Instead I found myself scared, and I had no idea what I wanted to do with my life. I met Ronnie and we decided to get married in October of 1967. Marriage is a challenge like no other challenge. Our marriage lasted for eight years. Our divorce took many people by surprise. The divorce was a very painful challenge. It was very humiliating to me and hard to face.

I began working in a factory in Mooresville. My foreman, Michael Burress, and I began dating. He was absolutely wonderful to me. Some of the employees enjoyed gossiping about us. That was quite an unusual challenge knowing your fellow workers were talking about you. Some of the employees had been speculating on what kind of girlfriend Michael would like. Well, they were surprised when they realized Michael and I were dating.

My younger sister Cathy died a few months after we had started dating. She was twenty-three years old. Cathy took her own life by overdosing on pills. She left behind three beautiful daughters. The oldest was five, and the twins were three. There wasn't anyone else to take care of them but me. This was something I sincerely wanted to do also. I had taken care of them for Cathy and grew to love them as if they were my own. They became a glorious blessing.

Michael and I were married right afterwards, on Christmas Day of 1975. We had a great marriage and Michael was fantastic with the girls. A few months after we were married my other sister Debbie phoned. She asked us if we wanted to take her four-month-old son to raise. This was quite a shock, and we just weren't sure. We knew we would love to have a son, but we did not want a lot of problems from Debbie. We told Debbie the only way would be if we could adopt him. Debbie agreed.

That same year we adopted all four children. Since our new son was so young, we decided to change his name. Michael and I renamed him David Michael Burress after his new dad, of course. Children give their parents all sorts of challenges, and ours were no different.

Instead of having a job outside our home, I babysat in our home. This way I could make the extra income we needed. I was good at what I did, and therefore word got around fast. At times I had to turn down people because I just had too many children. Having a daycare in my home was an interesting challenge. All the children and their parents were so different. I watched children from one month old to thirteen years old. I have now worked at my daycare for seventeen years. May of 1993 will be the last month of my daycare. I have enjoyed it tremendously even with all its difficult challenges. At this time in my life I do believe it is time to quit.

Michael and I were married for twelve years when he became extremely ill. Michael had an aneurysm that put him into Methodist Hospital for one month. He suffered greatly. I had never been around anyone that sick before. Watching someone you love being in so much pain was unbearable. The doctors took me into a little room several times to tell me that they did not believe Michael would pull through. I refused to give up hope. I could not imagine life without Michael. This was the hardest thing in the whole world for me to go through. I hope and pray I never ever have to go through anything even close to it again.

Michael was in a coma for a while, and he was operated on twice. There were a few hours that it appeared Michael was going to get better. During these few hours Michael and I shared a very special intimate time. I will cherish that special time forever. Michael developed pneumonia and had blood clots in his legs. The doctors found that he was bleeding internally in his stomach. When they operated on his stomach, he never recovered at all. During the operation they found blood clots floating everywhere. Afterwards Michael was what the doctors called brain dead. The doctors again took me into a little room to talk to me. This time the doctors wanted to know if I wanted to sign a paper to take Michael off the life-support machines. The doctors told me that Michael would never come out of the coma because of being brain dead. I said I would, but first I wanted a little time alone with Michael. Michael and I had talked about being on the life-support machines, and I knew he did not want to stay on them. I knew also that he would never come out of this and eventually die. I began talking to Michael even though I knew he could not hear me. The tears just kept streaming down my face. I loved him so very much.

As I was rubbing his forehead and arms, the truth really struck me. From the beginning of his illness the doctors thought he would die. They couldn't believe he was still hanging on to life. They even called him a miracle at times. Now it was obvious to me. Michael was leaving us to go to the place we call heaven, but he did not want to go. Michael did not want to leave his family because he loved us so much. It was strange in a way because Michael was the one person who taught us about God and Heaven. Michael had made me see that there was a real purpose for us in life and that God was real and alive. I could not understand the purpose for Michael dying and leaving us, though. Michael had taken such good care of us. The children and I were always first with Michael. All of a sudden I knew Michael was trying to hang on as long as possible because he was worried about us. He did not know how we would get along by ourselves.

I then began to tell Michael something that hurt so very, very deeply. I barely got the words out between all my tears and the love I felt for him. These are the words I spoke: "Michael, I love you with all my heart. I can feel the awful pain you are in. The children and I do not want you to leave us. Michael, you mean the world to us. We want you to know that if this is your time to go to heaven, then we want to let you go in peace. I just know you are trying to hang on because you are worried about us. You do not know how we will make it without you. We sure don't know either. Michael, we will make it, though, because you taught us to be so strong. We will make it just for you. Now go on to heaven ahead of us, rest, and somehow let us know what heaven is like. When our time comes, we will be ready and anxious to see you again."

Like a sign from God, all at once the machines began to go off, all at the same time. I will not forget the sad noise. Michael had died. I knew God was right there with us. I had let Michael go in peace, knowing we would be all right and knowing how much we dearly loved him. I never had to sign that paper the doctors told me about either. This was a horrible challenge that I wish everyone could avoid forever. The thought that someone each day somewhere is going through a similar challenge is heartbreaking. It is extremely painful. Michael had died on Sunday, May 29, 1988.

The funeral, I suppose, was my next challenge in life. We got through it though with the help of our family, friends and the sweet spirit of God.

Having to deal with everything myself was the next challenge I had to go through. I had to deal with the children and all the debts we owed. I had to keep on working in my daycare also. I usually went to bed scared and got up scared. I worried about the children, especially how they were dealing with the death of their dad. They were all so very close to Michael. I often felt they loved their dad so much more than me. It was as if he was their idol. All I seemed to hear was how great Dad was and if he was here things would be different. This time in my life was very lonely and hard to deal with. It did seem I was left to take care of everything myself. At times I did not do so well at making decisions either. I constantly worried about how I would fix something such as the car. I wondered what would happen if I got sick and could no longer work. As time went on I learned just how much the children did love me. We also got through whatever problems arose.

I have always regretted not going to college. Michael wanted to send me, but we decided with four children and so many debts, we would have to wait. It has been four and a half years since Michael died. I am now attending college at I. V. Tech in Bloomington. My children have showed me so much love and support. Also, I have a new man in my life that gives me such strength, support, hope, and, most of all, love. I thought I would never fall in love again. I am so glad to have been wrong. The new man in my life has helped me to realize it is time to give up my daycare. He has given me the courage to go back to school after twenty-five years. Hopefully I will achieve my dream of graduating from college. I am finding it is hard to study again after all these years. There is a lot of joy and fulfillment in trying. With all the love and support from my children and the new man in my life, I know without a doubt that I will reach my goals. By the way, the new man in my life is Ray Shepard. I never want to be without him. I know I am blessed, for I have found another true love. I do love him with all my heart. When graduation day comes, my children and Ray will be very proud of me as I will be of myself.

Kimberly S. Baird

Finding my way back to school was nothing less than a steep upward climb. Beginning in my first year of high school, depression became a prevalent part of my life. That was over nine years ago. Never did I anticipate that my life would take the direction it has. Depression has been only one of several factors of my emotional and mental health I have had to overcome; however, through great determination I fought to triumph above them all.

The journey through high school was difficult enough, and, with the compounded hindrance of chronic depression and low self-esteem, I sought to find understanding and acceptance in anyone. Coming from a background of neglect and abandonment by my parents, I had little sense of my own identity and would often drift from person to person and group to group, looking for a connection. Occasionally I was relieved of the emptiness within me; however, it was only temporary. Unfortunately, I turned to suicide on two occasions, which commenced counseling sessions with the pastor of my church. Eventually, through much parental pressure, I also became involved in the youth organizations of the church. My spirits began to lift, and I was making good Christian friends. Soon I was very active in the church. However, in time the pressure of having to be perfect was becoming wearying, as well as witnessing the hypocrisy of my own parents. I began to pull away from my Christian friends and quickly catapulted into drugs and alcohol. Throughout the following years I fluctuated from burying myself in religion to using chemicals to maintain my denial and numb the emotional pain I was experiencing.

Upon graduation I had little direction; however, in the years to come, that would be the least of my problems. I spent one summer in Chicago as a nanny for a wealthy family. In a short time I had met a few other nannies in the area. One girl, Jeannie, set me up on a blind date with a man whom she had just met. I was seventeen, naive, and with little dating experience, so I accepted. Unfortunately, by the end of the

Colorado Mountain College
3000 County Road 114
Glenwood Springs, CO 81601

25

date I had been sexually assaulted, and three years passed before I ever told anyone of the events that took place that night.

Meanwhile, I returned home to Michigan to attend college in Grand Rapids. The first semester was very productive, and I enjoyed my classes. However, by the second term I had taken a turn for the worse. Working part-time and taking a heavy load at school was taking its toll, as were the problems I was having with my parents. I moved in with a friend, and inevitably my substance abuse increased, but my attendance in class did not. At the same time I began an obsession with dieting, which later developed into full-blown bulemia. While the weight was shedding from me, I still continued to put 100% into my activities. I had not dropped out of college and was attending a vocational skills/trade center, cramming a two-year program into one year and working at a new job. Obviously, I couldn't maintain such a life style for very long and sought counseling with the pastor of my church once again. In addition to counseling, at my pastor and his wife's request I moved in with them. He was concerned with the fact that I was living alone in my parents' house while they were in Florida for the winter. During my stay at my pastor's, my moods were inconsistent and the suicidal feelings within me had not subsided. I began to seek help from a psychiatrist and was put on medications, which seemed to offer no relief. Although I had developed some sense of acceptance from my pastor's family, my pastor took advantage of my instability and began to sexually abuse me. This became the ultimate betrayal, and even though he would apologize and demand my forgiveness, his behavior reflected no sign of remorse since the abuse did not cease. In the next few weeks, I fought to put my idealized family back together in my mind, but guilt and shame overwhelmed me, and suicide became the only out that I could see. This attempt was far more serious than any previous attempt, and I found myself hours later in an emergency room hooked to various tubes and wires.

After transferring to a psychiatric hospital, I found my two-month stay did not bring any quick cures. Three weeks passed before I finally revealed that I had been sexually abused by my pastor. At that time my church and several friends there withdrew their support and encouragement. This was a difficult blow and hurt me deeply. Although my pastor ultimately did resign upon request, initially, I felt as though they disregarded his actions and blamed me. Due to an increasing distrust of others and fear of letting myself be vulnerable, I was noncompliant with therapy. I obtained little control over my eating disorder and additionally developed self-mutilation behaviors to further cope with the internal emotional distress I was under. Upon discharge I had gained only a superficial sense of stability, which would result in further hospitalizations.

When I was hospitalized for the third time, almost a year later, I desperately wanted to work through the sexual abuse, but was more reluctant to confront such issues as the neglect and abandonment from my parents. I was afraid of further rejection and alienation from them. At this point I had developed a serious drinking problem and turned to Alcoholics Anonymous at the request of a friend. Unfortunately, it was for my friend, not me, that I went and gained little from the program. However, I still made some effort at not drinking because I knew I had a problem. Following my discharge I was placed in an adult foster care home where I spent nearly two years. There I could be better observed and have medications dispensed on a daily basis, which reduced the risk of an overdose during this difficult time of adjustment. Despite the more protective environment, I still required further hospitalizations. My medications had never been fully stabilized and were frequently being increased, decreased, or discontinued. It was additionally frustrating dealing with uncomfortable and embarrassing side effects such as tremors, memory lapses, and agitation. During this time, therapy was at an intensely emotional and confusing level as I was working through many of my issues, as well as accepting that I have the mental illness called bipolar disorder, which is the more recent term for manic-depressive illness. Often I would find myself just trying to get through 10-15 minutes at a time without hurting myself in some way. My self-esteem was very low, and I had an abundance of anger directed at myself for being defective.

Fortunately, through much trial and error, the right combination of medication for me was achieved and my illness was getting under control. Furthermore, with the continuous support, encouragement, and dedication of my therapist and doctors, a small glimmer of hope was beginning to emerge.

In a short time that glimmer of hope expanded, and I developed a strong desire to make something of my life. I began to set goals to return to college, move out on my own, and start living again, maybe even for the first time. Also, the more I chose to take charge of my life, the more self-confidence I developed.

Now that I have reached those goals, I have established an entirely new set of educational goals. It is my intent to pursue the field of psychology so that I may give to others that which was given to me:

support, encouragment, unconditional care, and most importantly, an empathetic ear. The challenges that await me are minimal when compared to any previous one. However, I am faced with a long road ahead of studies. Nevertheless, within my heart lies a bountiful quantity of determination and motivation to continue to work until I reach my goals.

Greg Francis

Alcoholism has ruined countless lives since the beginning of time. It is a cunning, baffling disease that lures millions to destruction. Sometimes the grip of alcohol is broken, and someone is set free. After years of alcohol abuse, I was granted a miracle. After I was taught to live without alcohol, I learned to take charge of my life.

My drinking career started at age thirteen. Alcohol gave me confidence and a feeling of euphoria. When I was drinking, I became witty and spontaneous. I remember thinking that it would be great if I could feel that good every minute of every day. Alcohol had me under its evil spell.

My parents monitored my activities closely, so I had to become efficient at creating situations that would allow me to drink. During my freshman year in high school, I would attend varsity sporting events just long enough to borrow dollar bills from five or six of my friends. I would then meet an older friend at a predetermined time and place to go out drinking in his car.

Without realizing it, I gradually began limiting my activities to those that involved drinking. I surrounded myself with people who drank as much as or more than I did. If someone questioned my drinking, I tried to avoid that person whenever possible. Alcohol was my best friend, and my life became a quest for a buzz.

When I was fourteen, I was arrested for underage drinking at a football game. I was not sorry for what I had done, and I didn't think about the loved ones whom I had hurt. I only cared about drinking without getting caught again. Alcoholics are crafty, and I usually managed to hide my drinking from my coaches and my parents, but not from everyone.

After my arrest, the father of one of my friends, a recovering alcoholic, tried to talk to me about getting help, but I didn't listen. I believed my only problem was people like him trying to run my life. I refused to believe I was an alcoholic, and no one could tell me otherwise.

High school sped by in a blur of parties and many drunk nights. Although I was arrested a couple more times, my punishments were light. In 1983, I graduated at the bottom of my class, even though my comprehension test scores were well above average. College was not for me, so I went to work.

Once I began working, I spent most of my money on alcohol. I started binges that lasted days and sometimes weeks. I often woke up in strange places and couldn't remember how I had gotten there. Each morning I examined my car for evidence of a collision the night before. I no longer drank to feel the euphoria that I had once experienced. I now needed alcohol to function properly and to relieve the terror I felt when I was sober. A shot and a beer in the morning would calm my hangovers enough for me to show up for work.

During the summer of 1986, my mother was diagnosed with cancer and given less than a year to live. I didn't use the time to comfort my mother and help my family. Because I was working two jobs, I used this as an excuse for not being around. Actually, when I was not at work, I was drinking. I was enslaved by alcohol, and the master demanded my full attention.

Mother died after six months. It is difficult to describe the guilt that haunted me. Her death caused me to realize the stranglehold that alcohol had on me. Although I was not strong enough to change, I hated what I had become. I lived less than a block away from my parents, and instead of visiting my mother, I chose to get drunk.

A year after my mother died, I was diagnosed with diabetes and was ordered to follow a strict diet that did not include alcohol. I wanted to stop drinking and was determined to do so. Actually I tried, but I couldn't defeat the urge to drink. Consequently, I felt weak and pathetic, which just led to another drink.

The combination of drinking and diabetes led to many brushes with death. Friends began to avoid me because they never knew when they would have to call an ambulance for me. Once a doctor told me that I had a death wish after he had pulled me from a coma. He was much closer to the truth than he realized.

In December of 1990, I was arrested for my third Operating While Intoxicated offense. Because I was convicted of a class D felony, I was sentenced to thirty days in jail. I also had to complete a sixty-day inpatient alcohol abuse treatment program as well as sixty days of in-home detention.

I had finally hit rock bottom. After twelve years of heavy drinking,

I was ready to give up. I lost my job as well as my self-respect and the respect of those I cared about. I felt as important as a lump of tobacco that someone had spit on a sidewalk. Although I never tried suicide, I didn't dismiss the idea either.

Then came my miracle! While I was incarcerated, I began attending Alcoholics Anonymous meetings that were conducted at the jail. Listening to the discussions, I noticed that the lives of the participants had been no different from mine. Their stories were not exactly the same, but the feelings of hopelessness and despair were identical. But now these men were happy. I wanted what they had.

After twenty-nine days, I was released from jail and ordered to go directly to New Directions in Lafayette, Indiana, for the treatment program. My head had finally cleared from a month away from alcohol, and I had a desire to keep it that way. Nervous but excited and hopeful, I entered the program.

Alcohol treatment was nothing like I had envisioned. First, the only females there were the cooks and a couple of counselors. Second, although therapy sessions were conducted in groups, I was shown no pity from my counselor or my peers. I was actually expected to take responsibility for my actions and for my recovery. The first two weeks were hell. I wasn't allowed to use the phone or to have visitors. I felt as if I were being attacked during group sessions. My counselor and peers, always brutally honest, confronted me about my behavior. For a while, I actually thought that jail was preferable.

As time went on, I began to realize that in order to have a successful recovery, both my attitude and behavior would have to change. Once I started listening to criticism with an open mind, I began to grow. As part of my treatment, I was given many writing assignments, and my counselor encouraged me. She said that I had talent and that I should develop it. As a result, I decided to pursue a college degree.

When I graduated from New Directions, I moved into a halfway house in Indianapolis. Because the halfway house required its residents to be employed, I had to live for a while at the Salvation Army until I found a job. It was very difficult to obtain employment because of my police record and the fact that my driver's license had been suspended. Finally I found work doing odd jobs for an oil company. Often I worked outside in freezing temperatures at physically difficult jobs, but I could pay the bills.

The next step was to find a way to go to college. I had heard that Vocational Rehabilitation Service would help with financial aid because alcoholism is considered to be a handicap. So I talked with a counselor who said that I was qualified to receive four years of schooling. I had to complete some psychological testing in order to determine the amount of brain damage I had received due to alcohol abuse. Fortunately, the tests found no brain damage and an above average intelligence. My miracle continued.

About two months later, when I had almost completed the admission process at Indiana University-Purdue University at Indianapolis, I was laid off from the oil company. I tried desperately to find new employment, but my efforts were in vain. Had I still been drinking, I would have crumbled under the pressure. But I was now sober, and I had faith that no matter what happened, God would help me through.

At this same time, my older brother drowned in a pond close to his home in Tennessee. The temptation to drink at the time of the funeral was intense. But thanks to God and what I had learned while in treatment, I stayed clean. I was able to grieve in a healthy manner, unlike when my mother passed away.

When I returned to Indianapolis, everyone was very supportive. For example, my landlord was patient about my rent. But I still couldn't find a job, and after six weeks my residency was terminated. At that point my father suggested I move back home with him. I quickly made the necessary phone calls and had everything transferred to Kokomo, where I now reside. This delayed the financial aid from vocational rehabilitation, but everything was in order for late registration at Indiana University at Kokomo by the fall of 1992.

I have just completed my first semester with a grade point average of 3.35, the best grades of my life. I hope to be a physical therapist and work with handicapped children. Since I also enjoy writing, I would like to incorporate it into my career.

There are still some hurdles to leap and bridges to cross. My driver's license will be suspended for another eight years, making it difficult to use the school facilities and cutting down on job prospects. Some of my required classes are offered only during the day, and my father, who is my chauffeur, works from 6 A.M. to 3 P.M. But these are problems with which I can cope.

I would not be where I am today if I had not been forced to view my life in an honest manner. Alcohol almost killed me many times, and I am still only one drink away from a life of hell. I have been sober for almost two years, and I have never felt happier or more serene. With God's grace, I will stay sober today. Tomorrow will take care of itself.

Regina Ruiz

I feel funny. So very funny, telling you about my life, my feelings, my secrets. I do not know how to welcome you into my heart and soul. You see, nobody ever asked me what I thought or how I felt about life's challenges. Or, maybe, they never really cared about what I thought.

My journey to Burlington County College began many years ago in Caracas, Venezuela, where I was born and grew to a young lady full of energy and life. My parents called me Regina because there was something regal about the sound. They had high hopes of my marrying a local boy from a good, wealthy family. You know the kind—slick, black hair, long sideburns, driving a sport car. The kind who brings you flowers on every date and swears his undying love for you three days a week, and the other days he is sleeping with Maria, the local social worker.

To get even, or because I was in a romantic haze, I met and married a U.S. Marine from Des Moines, Iowa, who was stationed at our local Embassy, where I also worked.

Marriage, a home in America, and three beautiful children occupied twenty-five years of my life.

Where did my life go? It went somewhere. But there is no lost and found department for a life lost in the years.

The marriage was bad. It was so bad that I cried every night for all those years. I would tell myself, "You are in a strange country—maybe the customs are different. The children need me and I cannot admit failure to my parents back in Venezuela."

As luck would have it, fate intervened. My ex-Marine husband found someone new and left me and the children with no money, very hurt and depressed.

I quickly took an inventory—foreign-born, with not a great command of the English language, no money, no job training and two kids in college. The future looked bleak.

But it did not stop. My father died. I loved him so much, and he was always my source of strength in need. Mother became ill.

I felt very hurt, lonely, angry, and very sorry for myself.

I remembered a saying my Dad would quote to me when things were going wrong and the future looked black. He may have gotten this quote from the Spanish edition of *Reader's Digest*. He would say, "My dear, it is always the darkest when you are fresh out of matches."

"Dad, I am out of matches." Or so I thought.

I decided to make my life something worthwhile by helping people. I wanted to help and heal. Maybe, at the same time, heal myself.

I appeared before the college doors with my knees shaking and full of doubt. I wanted to be a nurse.

I enrolled in college. I was proud of myself for not falling into the garbage pit waiting so close by.

Then the fun began—subjects which were very hard for me.

In order to survive, I managed to get two jobs to keep up with house payments and food. The kids found college money by working and appealing to their father.

I met my challenge on a daily basis. Now, my days begin long before the sun makes its appearance. I stumble bleary-eyed to the shower and afterwards select the day's outfit. After a quick check in the mirror, I make my way downstairs to prepare a quick breakfast along with my lunch, feed the cat (who happens to be my alarm clock), and do what seems like a million other small chores. Then I drive for forty-five minutes to the Pemberton Campus, while studying my chemistry key notes on index cards before a test. I would do this with tears in my eyes. You see, at the same time I am worrying about the situation with my water heater that slowly but surely is leaking and may not last until the new one can be installed. In addition, I am anxious to schedule my exterminator's visit to treat the termites discovered in my basement. My preoccupation with such household woes is due to a cancelled appointment to have my furnace cleaned, which resulted in a periodic spray of soot.

After a hectic morning of classes, I rush to my car for a hurried thirty-minute ride to the office, where a desk piled high with import documents is waiting for me, along with innumerable phone calls from the brokers, custom officials and suppliers. Meanwhile, an impatient boss wants to know the precise location of one of the fifty containers traveling between eastern Europe and Burlington, New Jersey.

As the clock winds toward 5:00 P.M., I get ready to travel back to the Cinnaminson Campus for another round of classes. As I arrive on campus, I waste another thirty minutes searching for that nonexistent parking spot. My class continues until 10:00 in the evening, and I praise the Lord it doesn't last longer. By that time, I am beginning to see double. I slowly make my way to the car and begin the long commute home, counting in my mind how many customers I will see as a result of my second job—hairdressing. On evenings when I have no classes scheduled, I take appointments to cut hair or give permanents. As I arrive home, I find a hungry son and starving cat, both waiting to be fed. I usually cook something simple for us, then proceed to do the few dishes because I hate the thought of adding one more chore to my early morning schedule. By the time I finish getting ready for bed, it is midnight; I look up and see the stairway leading to the bedroom, which by then seems longer than the one outside the Philadelphia Museum of Art, and proceed to crawl in bed and into the arms of Morpheus.

People question the wisdom of my studying to be a nurse. It may take four or five years.

"You will never last," they tell me.

"You will be too old to lift a bed pan," they mock.

But I am not discouraged. There are twenty more courses ahead of me before I get into the nursing area. While all these things challenge me, the greatest of all is to be able to hold my head high.

Somehow, just somehow, I think it might be all worth it—if I can hold the hand of someone dying all alone in a cold hospital ward and whisper in their ear, "You are not alone, I am here, I am here, I will never leave you."

Maybe, just maybe, I will find that life that was lost. It is out there somewhere.

But I know one thing—"I am in charge," and I will never let go again. Never.

Regina Lynn Rayder

I am thirty-eight years old, and I just completed my first semester at Roane State Community College. I passed with a grade point average of 4.0. I have had to overcome many obstacles along the way in order to get to where I am today. I am also looking forward to my next semester in January.

To begin with, I was unable to attend high school because I had been expelled for disruptive behavior when I was in junior high school. I had staged a riot because girls were not allowed to attend school wearing slacks. I had to walk about four miles to school every day, and I would get so cold that my bare legs would chap and bleed, and so I refused to wear a dress. I was expelled from school because I started wearing slacks and had gotten many of the other girls to follow my example. As a result, the rest of the students sided with me and refused to return to school. All the students in school couldn't be expelled, so we had won the battle. We were allowed to wear slacks. There was other disruptive behavior from me also. For example, I would sometimes take food from the cafeteria because my family was very poor and I never had enough to eat. The one free meal a day that I would eat at school was all I would have until the next meal the following day. When I would get caught, I got a paddling and would have to stay after school for a week as punishment. I was very skinny and I had to be at school every day in order to eat, so I would try and take my mind off the hunger pains by concentrating on learning. I made good grades and was looking forward to high school, but I was not allowed to attend. When I went to register for high school, the principal called me into his office and said because of my disruptive behavior in junior high school that I would not be accepted.

I left school and studied on my own and was able to obtain a General Equivalency Diploma. The next step on my agenda was to go to college. I was twenty years old, and I had made all the necessary preparations in order to attend. I had taken the entry exam, which I passed, and had gotten my schedule for classes.

When I arrived home from the college that day, a deranged man was waiting on me. He had been stalking me for a year and had raped me a few months before. He put me out of commission for the next three weeks. When he first raped me in July of seventy-five, I had become pregnant. Near the last week in October he broke into my home to rape me again, and he shot me through the chest and through the left wrist. I was in the hospital in intensive care for eight days. My left lung had collapsed from the .357 Magnum bullet that had penetrated it. The baby that I was pregnant with was four months matured and threatening to miscarry. I was hemorrhaging so much that I had to receive many blood transfusions. As a result, I was very weak, and it would take me about a year to regain the use of my left arm.

He raped me two weeks after my baby was born and would continue to rape me periodically for the next four years. He was always very brutal, and he always used a gun. It was impossible for me to escape this man because he was best friends with the city judge, who was very powerful, and anything he did was always "taken care of." I had called the Tennessee Bureau of Investigation, but somehow the judge found out about the call and I was "persuaded" to keep my mouth shut. Between him and the judge and a few men on the police force, I didn't have a chance. I confided in a man I knew about what was happening to me, and he tried to help. He protected me for about a month before they shot him in the back one night. I was forced to go with the murderer to get rid of the gun. The murder is still on record as unsolved. I wanted to talk with the Federal Bureau of Investigation, but I never did because they hurt me so badly when I talked with the Tennessee Bureau of Investigation. Since they found out I had talked about it, I didn't know who I could trust.

I was still trying to get an education, and I was accepted into a nursing program at an area vocational school. I had finished about four months when the rapes started again. This man was insane, and I was trapped. He would do a lot of crazy things such as put one bullet in the gun and spin the chamber, then hold it against my head and pull the trigger. He would beat me and handcuff me to the bed and put a piece of cloth in my mouth and tie another around my head to keep that one in. I was afraid I would vomit and drown or that I would start to cry and my nose would stop up so I wouldn't be able to breathe. He would keep me like this for hours while he raped and tortured me, and he would describe in detail how he was going to kill me. I was beginning to miss school because he would sometimes play his sick games for days. I was finally dismissed from school because I missed too many days. (Six months of training "down the drain" left me devastated.)

I decided to make another attempt to get away from this man. I wanted to live so badly, but I couldn't endure any more of his torture. The next time he pushed his way into my home and put the gun to my head, I calmly turned and walked out of the door. He had hit me with the gun, I suppose, because I was bleeding and my vision had blurred. He yelled for me to stop or he would kill me. I just kept walking. I heard him cock the gun, and I felt the bullet as it whizzed past my head. I expected at any moment for him to shoot me in the back, but I just kept walking. He fired the gun again as I opened my car door, and I got in and drove away. I got married a month after that incident, to a man I hardly knew and didn't care anything about. I just didn't want to be by myself when that monster came back. I was twenty-five years old.

When I turned thirty-three, I was on my own again with four children and no way to support them. I turned to government assistance and was trying to get into a position to attempt college again. Finally, after five years, my youngest child was in school and I had saved enough money for a used car. I was finally able to attend college. Now I look forward to everything, and I am determined to make my life better. I also want to help my children become productive adults. I watched my oldest child graduate last year, and my sixteen-year-old will graduate this year. My eight- and nine-year-old children have made the honor roll at school every year. I do all I can to ensure that they are intellectually motivated. For example, my nine-year-old has taken a computer class for a month each summer for the last two years. My sixteen-year-old volunteers as a substitute teacher a few hours a week during her study time at school. She has access to all the computers and other machines and knows how to operate them. I take her to the college I attend on Saturdays, and she has taught me all she knows about the computer. We study at the library, and she helps me "brush up" on using the different indexes and the different machines. She does a lot of her school work at the college, and when she goes to college this fall, she will be familiar with the surroundings.

Finally, I am where I want to be, and I look forward to each day. I don't worry about the man who raped me because I haven't seen him in thirteen years, and the judge who protected him is dead. All of the obstacles I have had to overcome in order to get to college have made me more determined to succeed. I am finally taking charge of my life.

Stacy Ebeling

I learned to fail as a small child. The lessons taught in my family had little to do with succeeding in school or life. I was a frail and petite girl who learned early that my ideas and perceptions were worthless. I remember a time coming home after school when I was in the fourth grade. I was wearing my brown and white checkered dress. I was the first one to arrive of the four children. My mother was sitting in the kitchen talking to a friend and sipping coffee. I set my school books on the kitchen table and greeted them. Mom turned and asked me, "Is the wall black or white?" She was pointing at our white kitchen wall. I replied, "The wall is white." She slapped my face. My cheek stung and tears filled my eyes. I looked to her friend, who stoically sat there and did nothing. At that moment, I tried to figure out what was happening. My mother then asked me again, "What color is the wall, Stacy?" Hurt and angry, I looked at her and said, "The wall is black." Mom looked at her friend and smiled. I picked up my school books and went to my room and cried. I learned in grade school that you do not challenge authority and that I was of little value.

My lessons in the classroom were sometimes as painful as they were at home. I have a twin sister who is developmentally disabled. She had always been in special education classes until our seventh grade year. She sat in the row to my right and one desk closer to the front of the classroom. Two boys sat in the same row with my sister, one of them in front of her and one behind her. We brought our lunches to school in a brown paper bag which we kept under our desks. On one occasion, the two boys began kicking Tracy's lunch back and forth between them. Tracy was too shy to stand up for herself. I was enraged that those boys were being mean to my sister. I whispered, "Stop it." The boy sitting beside me smashed her lunch with his foot and laughed at me. He then kicked her lunch back to his friend. I yelled, "Stop it!" The teacher had been writing on the blackboard with her back to the class. I heard her call my name: "Stacy, go to the back of the room."

She grabbed a big ruler and followed me to the rear of the classroom and told me to bend over and put my hands on a table. She hit me three times while the class watched. She never asked me what happened. That day I was humiliated in school.

I went to five different high schools because my family moved so frequently. I don't recall anyone at school ever telling me what needed to be done to prepare to go on to college. No one ever helped me pick out classes. When I was sixteen and a sophomore in high school, my mother told me that I was smart enough to go to college. That same year, she and my stepfather bought me a new Ford Pinto. I sometimes drove friends to lunch off campus. On a fall afternoon, I came home right after school and was met by my mother. The first thing she said to me was, "There was a black boy in the back seat of your car today." I had taken three friends to lunch, and one of them was black. She took the car keys, and I no longer had a car. I was never allowed to drive a family vehicle again. Shortly after this, she kicked me out of the house. Survival was in and college was out.

After living with a teacher and his family for one year, I was allowed to move back home. My current stepfather was my first real father figure. He was the third stepfather, but he was also my first hope for a father. One Saturday night, we were downstairs sitting together watching television. He made a pass at me. I was frightened. I told my brother, hoping he would protect me. He confronted my stepfather, who in turn told my mother. I had just graduated from high school, and Mother kicked me out again. She didn't believe my story. Not long after that I was married.

My husband had achieved all of his goals. He was satisfied with where he was in life. I worked off and on to supplement our income. We both came from dysfunctional backgrounds where higher education was not a value. We repeated our programmed histories with each other and found our way to divorce court nine years later. I found myself alone with my four-year-old son. I met a male friend who tried to talk me into going to college. He wanted me to go to school. I wasn't ready. Financially and personally, the idea seemed impossible.

I had never been taught to plan ahead. Long-term goals were not part of my existence. I had been a victim my entire life and had no insight into my condition. Depression and the resulting lack of self-esteem and self-confidence had become a way of life. There was no place in my life for school. Anyway, I was scared that I could fail again. I could feel as worthless as I did in our kitchen when I was in the fourth grade, or as humiliated as I was at the back of the room in the seventh grade, or as alone as I did when I was kicked out of my home.

I had a job selling janitorial supplies for a company that offered no security or potential for advancement. The owner never kept his promises regarding commissions and salary. I hated my job. I began to feel desperate. I was forced to stop and look in the mirror. Who was I? I was thirty-two years old and I had no identity, no real direction, and no purpose in my life. I wanted to lock myself up in my house and stay there. Something had to change. I had to take a risk. My male friend stood by me and encouraged me. I went to therapy. My therapist also encouraged me. I called the local college. I still didn't have the courage to go to the school yet. Two months later I called the college again. This time I made an appointment at the Learning Skills Center. It was tough for me to take that first step.

The staff wanted me to take some tests. The thought scared me. I never excelled in school. I had not learned to value education. For the first time I wanted to do well, yet I feared failure. I took tests to explore my interests and to uncover what I was capable of doing at the collegiate level. The staff told me I was not ready to take on the courses offered without more preparation. These educators gave me an identity. I became an "adult returning student." I was one of the new generation seeking an education.

Sitting in class the first day was like being a kid again, but there I was in an adult body. My pencil was rolling back and forth between my fingers nonstop! My foot tapped throughout that first class as if it had an independent source of energy. I lived through the first day of school.

It was quickly apparent that I did not know how to study. The faculty had the foresight to see that I was enrolled in a class entitled "College Success." This teacher was dedicated to instilling new skills in me that would ready me to face the world of academia. I needed to learn how to take notes, read a professor in order to succeed in any particular class, manage my time efficiently, prepare for tests, and successfully cope with stress in school.

The word "stress" does not adequately describe what came next. My ten-year-old son began to share me with textbooks. Suddenly, he was in competition with college prep math and a writing skills course. Cooking dinner, doing laundry, vacuuming the house, and paying bills also had to compete with these new demands on my limited resources. My social life died. Refusing to bury it entirely, I joined a support club at school. The group had dubbed itself ANTS for Adult Non-Traditional

Students. I made new friends whose confidence in me exceeded my own. Just before the end of that first semester, they elected me president for the following school year. I had developed a desire to learn and to succeed. I was sure that I would barely pass two of my first three classes. When straight "A's" came in, I was ready to celebrate.

That semester was just the beginning. Next, it was on to courses like Introductory Algebra and English 101. A new wave of anxiety and fear swept over me. Furthermore, how was I going to stand up in front of the ANTS group and actually lead a meeting? Without realizing it, I took on the philosophy of a recovering alcoholic. I was now taking one day at a time. As the semester progressed, I maintained the attitude of giving my best effort. Some tests didn't go as well as others. I'd just do better on the next one. I was now a student. I was putting direction in my life. I had a future, in spite of my past!

I have not reached the summit of this peak yet. The economic recession discussed on the nightly network news is nothing compared to the financial dilemmas I face daily as a single parent in college. My child's new Cub Scout shirt meant careful sale shopping for that month's necessities. We will continue to carefully manage other resources as well in the years ahead before the sheepskin is in hand. Quality time with my child is a major objective enroute to the top of this mountain. I want an education to be as important to him as it now is to me. My desire is to succeed for both of us. He now brings his homework to the kitchen table and we work together.

The top of this mountain will be finishing my training as a physical therapist. However, this climb will not be my last; it is the preparation for many more to come. My intellectual, emotional, and spiritual growth is a lifelong endeavor. I plan to share my success by sharing my story and my skills with others. I learned to fail as a child, and I am learning to succeed as an adult.

Ruby Rolon

In 1953 on the 31st of May, I was born. I had beautiful parents who loved me and helped me to grow into a person I liked very much. But on June 8, 1964, my father died. That began a whole new life for me. It was a life that I hope no child would ever have to live through, though I believe millions of children do.

Things seem to change when there is a death in the family. You experience feelings you never knew existed in you, such as anger, jealousy, hurt, fear, and loneliness. You don't just feel these things; you start acting them out. So it was in my case.

My mother began drinking heavily after my father's death. She would stay out all night, leaving the six of us alone to take care of ourselves. I thought we did pretty well. We could go anywhere, do anything. We didn't have any supervision at all.

I missed my mother. She wasn't the mother that got up every morning and made us breakfast. She wasn't the mother that helped decorate Valentine boxes or bake cookies for us anymore. I remember my brother and me sharing a can of peas. I hated peas! But I learned to eat them because no one cooked.

I longed for my mother's attention. I wanted her to see that I was growing into a young woman, but that didn't seem very important to her. She wanted the alcohol. We were second to her.

One of my sisters had married before Mom's drinking became heavy. I was glad, because she wouldn't have to live like we did. She would be taken care of. I wanted to be loved too, most of all by my mother, but she could not separate herself from the bottle.

My older brother was thirteen at the time my mother began drinking. By sixteen, he had been in trouble with the police, had stolen things, and God only knows what else went on in his life. Before his seventeenth birthday, he took a gun from someone and killed himself.

How alone he must have been. How hurt and afraid he must have been of life. I never had a chance to tell him I loved him. I never had a chance to really know him. I wanted to know him more because he had grown into a person that you couldn't really understand. He was hardly ever home, and when he was, it was just briefly. I loved him, no matter what he thought of me.

Life went on for the rest of us. I existed, though not really wanting to. I hated life. What was the reason for it? I saw no reason, no hope, no happiness. I HATED LIFE!

At sixteen, I decided I would quit school. Quitting was something I had to do but didn't really want to do. The peer pressure was too much for me. I had been ridiculed and humiliated too many times about my clothes, my size, and my hanging out alone. I had no friends because no one wanted to get close to me.

Mom hadn't paid the bills, so the utilities had been cut off. We washed our clothes by the side of the road at night. I don't remember how we cleaned our bodies. I think we had cold water, but I'm not sure. I just know that I didn't look nice or smell nice when I went to school. Mom never noticed. I wished she would have.

She did notice when I wanted to get married at eighteen. I had never had a boyfriend, so I married the first man that asked me. I thought that I loved him, but I realized I just used him to escape that life of alcohol and misery. I never meant to hurt him. I never wanted to hurt anyone, ever.

I met another man that I thought could really make a difference in my life. He did make a big difference. I wanted to commit suicide. He didn't love me. No one would ever love me! Why should I live?

I drank two bottles of pills. I was very tired of trying to get love. I didn't know any other way. Not being loved hurt very much. I couldn't take any more hurting from anyone. I just wanted to die.

It didn't happen. I don't know why; it just didn't work. Someone took care of me while I was "out." It wasn't the man I lived with. I awoke to find that I was pregnant.

I had tried so hard before to get pregnant. If I only had a child! Someone I could love, someone to love me! Now I had a chance at life. I had a reason to live again! I knew that baby would be special. I just knew it!

I stayed another year with this baby's father. I had grown somehow. I knew I had to be a responsible person. This was a life that I held in my hands. He was not going to be abandoned; he would not go hungry or go around dirty. He was special. Above all, he was loved.

I have married since then, and I have three children more. I'm very blessed with my children. I don't have everything I need for my children, but they're very much loved. I'm trying to go to college now at thirty-nine years old. I've made this decision even though there are still many obstacles in my way. For example, I don't have the full support of my husband, although I wish I did. My children and I are going through trying times, but no one said it would be easy.

I'm determined to make it through because when I think of my past, I think of their future. I also think of all the children in this world that are going through what I went through! I want to be there, if only for just one of them. As a social worker, maybe I can help save some child from a life full of hurt. I will make it through college and be a social worker because I am taking charge of my life! Then I can help others to make a difference.

Kevin Shawn Watkins

How does a person overcome the feeling that he or she never accomplished what they were capable of doing in life? The feeling that they could have done more or been more, if only circumstances were different? I've always wanted to attend college and test myself in hopes of a better future for my family and myself. But environmental, economical, physical, and mental obstacles would delay my taking charge of my life.

First of all, I came from an environment that included a dysfunctional family. My father was, and still remains, an alcoholic who abandoned his family. His influence on my life was anything but good. My mother raised four children on her own and turned to prescription drugs to cope with life. Neither parent was able to instill the values of an education, even though I understood the importance of having one. I remember coming home with my report card and grinning from ear to ear with all A's. But when I arrived the house was empty; Mom wasn't home from work yet. I would sit on the front porch and wait and wait. Finally, when she drove up, I would rush to show her what I'd done. After showing her my grades, she would say, "Honey, you did great, but I've had a hard day and need to lie down." That kind of took all the air out of my balloon. Every other year my father would drive up to see how much we had grown. I wasn't that enthused about showing my report card to someone who reeks of Jack Daniels.

School became a refuge from my home life. I enjoyed the attention the teachers gave me for doing well on my assignments. They always had a kind word to say about me. I thought to myself, someday I want to go to college and become a teacher. Teachers not only asked questions, but they also had answers. They were adults that people looked up to, and I was proud of them. Honestly, they probably thought I was a pest. I was always asking questions and volunteered for any project. But they never discouraged me from participating. Somehow they must have known my situation at home and the rough road ahead of me.

My environment changed to economic poverty. My parents' divorce was final, and my father either forgot or ignored his child support payments. We were now official welfare recipients. I'll never forget the embarrassment I felt paying for groceries with food stamps while my friends from school stood behind me in line. I was a teenager now and determined to get an education and never live this nightmare again. I was a straight A student, and nothing was going to stop me. Little did I know that life was fixing to hit me like a Patriot missile. Our home was confiscated by the government for back taxes. Our next stop was the projects and a four-room shack. To help my mother and family, I started working part-time on construction sites. One year later I was a high school dropout and a full-time employee. My dreams of college were gone, and I knew there was no turning back. I was still determined to be the best at what I was doing, so at nineteen I became the youngest foreman with the construction company I worked for. I taught myself to read blueprints and never missed an opportunity to voice an opinion or new idea. My teachers at school had taught me well. Five years later I hit a brick wall. This was as far as I go without a degree. There were no openings in our offices for dropouts. I was destined for construction sites the rest of my career, or worse yet, the rest of my life.

Next, I went into a mental depression and started to blame my father and everyone else for destroying my life. I was a victim of society and all its cruel ways. So, in a last-ditch effort to salvage myself, I decided to test for my GED. I went to Texas Christian University and passed on my first try. I felt proud and my dreams returned. I could now do anything I set my mind to. This became a short-term victory, for I was now an alcoholic and addicted to cocaine. I was following in my parents' footsteps. I was using drugs and alcohol to cope with life.

Work became extremely demanding. Part-time school was out of the question. Business was booming and we had jobs all over Dallas and Fort Worth. Exxon, J. C. Penney's, and GTE were moving their corporate headquarters to the area. American Airlines and Delta were expanding at DFW airport. There was no way I could leave my job and the money it provided. The work grew into seventy hours and enormous amounts of cocaine and alcohol. I was now trapped in a revolving door. If not for the help of a woman named Belinda, I would have died.

After five years that I have little memory of, I flew to Springdale, Arkansas. There I checked into a Drug and Alcohol Recovery program called Decision Point. After ninety days there, I finally reached a point to make the decision to turn my life around. I also came to believe and trust in the God Belinda told me about. After leaving Decision Point I married Belinda. Life was great, my dream was back, and I was going to go to college. I never dreamed of another brick wall I had no control over.

Mentally I had picked up the pieces, but physically something had gone wrong. My left arm and half of my left hand had gone numb. Belinda told me to see a doctor, but I told her we would pray and wait. Two weeks later I was in the hospital emergency room. Instead of getting better, the muscles in my hand had deteriorated. Because of repetitive use of hand tools, my tendons had swelled and destroyed the nerves in my arm. After two surgeries I am now legally handicapped.

With Belinda's courage and our trust in God, we found an organization that helps handicapped people retrain for new work. They tested me and said they could help me attend a two-year college. My dream was still achievable. I chose radiology to tackle for a new career.

I am attending Tarrant County Community Junior College. The anxiety is unbelievable but exciting. For instance, besides remedial English I am also taking remedial math. I had trouble spelling *algebra*, let alone working the equations. They allow a student two tests on each chapter. The better grade of the two tests the student can keep. I studied hard for the first test and was ready to take it—I thought. I scored a 54 percent, an F. I was really worried and thought maybe seventeen years away from school were too many. But Belinda and prayer showed me back to the books. I studied all weekend and was ready again Monday morning. I scored a 95 percent, an A. A person would have thought I had just won the lottery. Even though I passed this semester with all B's, I realize the hard work involved. Every semester requires the same hard work and more. I have a second chance at life that most people never get and understanding that is a must for me. I can return to the nightmare I came from by forgetting exactly where I came from.

Although a child may come from a terrible environment, or extreme poverty, or have physical or mental problems, he or she is still special. And with the help of a loving God and some very special loving people, each child has a chance to take charge of their own life.

Mary K. Vant

I was sixteen years old when I left home to take charge of my life. I had explained to my parents that I was not running away; that I was simply on a quest to find myself. Taking a Greyhound bus ride across the country to Arizona, I managed to avoid pimps, get healed by a schizophrenic and meet Miss Third Place New York State. These three adventurous days on the bus confirmed my independence. Being a "rebel without a cause," I knew I had "the world by the balls." I wanted to "take a walk on the wild side," to live the "rough and tumble life" of the biker, and I wanted everything now! Little did I know at that time that the path I had chosen would have a tremendous impact on my life today.

A year later when I had returned home from Arizona, I tried to finish out my last two years of high school at St. Vincent Pollatti. I managed to make it through the first year without getting expelled until the last three days. Furiously, I was told by the principal, "Take your final exams, get the hell out of here and don't come back!" I guess we just did not see eye to eye on various things. Passing all of my exams, I left the school, never returning to finish my senior year. My mom had a friend who was a priest who could have interceded on my behalf, but I refused to go back because of my false pride. Inevitably I was finding excuses to stay home from school, and my attendance was rare. This was a relief to my teachers, although one teacher from elementary school told me years later, "Kate, you were a rotten kid, but you were a cute rotten. I miss you." The following summer after leaving school I discovered the world of construction.

Starting at $5.00 per hour as a carpenter's helper, I knew then that money was worth more than an education. This job was meant for me. I could get high with the foreman, drink during and after work, and best of all, I did not have to think to do my job. Every day I was just going through the motions of carrying lumber from one pile to the next and slamming nails. These simple functions came naturally. From that point on I did not want anything to do with anything unless it involved a hammer and nail.

This was my world; and, through sheer determination, I enfeebled my mind and was able to attain the lofty level of a street-wise punk kid. If I were to learn anything, it would have to be about residential or commercial construction; otherwise I had no interest. I refused to read or listen to the news, and politics was beneath my dignity. If I watched television, it would have to be *The Flintstones*. I was in the Stone Age and pretty much stoned. The most important things in my life were a paycheck on Friday and a party until the money ran out.

One morning I was lying in bed glassy-eyed, afraid to move my head in fear that the intense pain would start banging away. The inside of my mouth felt like I had just eaten a bag of sawdust. Carefully I turned my head to stare at the bald man lying next to me. He was almost twice my age, and it seemed as though he was losing a different tooth each day. I was frightened of the first thoughts that ran through my head. Staring at this man, all I could think of was "Good God! Am I going to have to take care of this man for the rest of my life? I can hardly take care of myself! Who is going to take care of me?" He too was in the field of construction and was never able to hold on to a job. Having no basis for a future, he was living paycheck to paycheck as I was. Looking at him even longer, I became disgusted with what he was and what I had become. I could build a house, but where was my home?

I was twenty-three when I finally realized the first life of partying and living paycheck to paycheck was not the way I wanted to live my life. This world that I had created for myself had become very stale and stagnant. My co-workers became a drag. Every day was a repeat of the day before. Who was the better carpenter? Who could talk the crudest while blowing snot out of one nostril and wiping the remains on their sleeves? Oh yes, let me not forget the usual talk about the women they had or could have had if they had pursued them. By this time the only thing I really enjoyed about my job was working with my hands, being able to stand back from the house I just finished and say, "I helped build that house!" Deep down inside I knew that I was only able to survive in this world because of my propensity to smoke grass, which allowed me to escape reality. Unrealistically, I thought that some day all my dreams would come true and that success would mysteriously fall into my lap. Although I dreaded construction, it was a love-hate relationship. There were days when I would trowel a building with two hands, sink a nail in two strikes, carry lumber on my shoulder as high as my arm could stretch, and walk the walls of buildings without the fear of falling. These were the only things I did well and felt good about. During the nine years of construction work, I had been foreman twice and had turned down a offer for a foreman's position. Even though I was capable of doing all these things, I realized I did not know the difference between condos and condoms. I had lost the desire to lead this kind of life because I had hit an impasse.

Feeling a strong need to break away from the life I had built for myself, I realized I would have to let go of a lot of myself that I did not like. Afraid of the unknown, I was hesitant to change the life to which I had become accustomed. Yet there was no chance of change if I continued to live the life I was leading. Slowly I began to straighten out my life. My so-called friends disapproved of my actions when I refused to partake in their nightly parties. They did not understand the sudden change, and I was forcefully harassed. Refusing to take this sitting down, I bounced back with just as much force because I felt my life was being threatened. They did not like the change they saw in me, and I did not like what I saw in them. Eventually my friendships became extinct due to the fact that I was not giving in and they were not going to change. During this time I lost my job and home. Working for myself, I barely made enough money to survive.

Coming to the point of having to choose to live in my truck or move back home with Mom and Dad, I decided to try and wheedle my way back into their home. It was almost winter, and it was beginning to get cold. First I attempted to talk to Mom. Before I could plead my case, she told me, "Kate, I will do anything possible to help you stay out of our house!" She had no idea what a bruise to my ego it was to ask her for help, and at the same time, I did not understand what she was trying to tell me. Turning to an alternative plan, I went to plead for help from Dad. Always having been Daddy's little girl, I managed to get back into their home with the pleading argument, "When I was sixteen, I left home and have not been back that much in the past seven years. I want to go back to school, paying my own way of course, but I need an affordable place to live in order to pay for my education. Please give me a chance to change." Running out of words, I tried to use humor, telling my Dad, "I left home when I was young, and you have missed out on seven years of my childhood; please let me give them back to you." As the tears dripped from my eyes, Dad said to me, "Kate, it breaks my heart to see you cry! You know you can always come home."

Never having lived any other way than the quick and easy life, I found it difficult to stay sober. Almost on the verge of giving up on my dreams of getting an education and a better life, I had to let go of my false pride and again reach out for help. Looking for guidance, I met a few people who were surprisingly willing to help me without any idea of who I was. With no hesitation they took me under their wings. I was skeptical of their motives at first. They told me if I wanted to change, I would need to stay clean and sober, taking "one day at a time." Repeatedly, these people gave me their telephone numbers and told me to call at any time. Absolutely convinced these people were crazy, I still called them, and to this day a few of these nuts are some of my closest friends. They helped me build my self-esteem, taught me how to live and have fun without partying, and constantly reminded me to be myself because they accepted me as I was. They taught me, through faith and hope, that everything will be okay, because today is the first day of the rest of my life, and that at any point during that day I can start over again.

Staying sober did not seem to be enough, and once again it was time for another change. The only chance I felt I had for advancement in my life was through getting an education. Knowing very little outside of carpentry, I had the desire to learn more about everything and anything I could.

I started to notice how ridiculous my street slang sounded when I would talk to people. Gradually, the dissatisfaction with my speech caused me to remember the great determination with which I chose all the undesirable paths in my life. I recalled my downfall in North Beach, Maryland. This was the only place I knew where there was a biker club where the bikers were all on foot, without bikes. When I lived in North Beach, it did not take too much for me to feel superior. Having all my teeth seemed to be enough. As I began to change, thoughts of this past at North Beach would send chills up my spine. Shaking away these thoughts, I began to think of my new goals. And while I dreamed of building my own house someday out in the country, it suddenly dawned on me that I could talk, dream, and pray all I wanted, but nothing would happen unless I got off my ass and did something about it.

During the fall of 1991 I went to Prince George's Community College to register for classes. I had a problem: all that I could think of was my prior history in school. Before I could go through the school doors again, I had to battle with all of the doubts that were plaguing my mind. I knew for sure someone would dig up my school records and tell me, "Miss Vant, there is no room in this college for any one as incorrigible as you!" To my relief, this did not happen. Trying to believe in myself, I would constantly tell myself over and over, "The past is the past, and being human, you will make mistakes." This was my opportunity to prove to myself that, if given the chance, I could change.

After registering for classes, I was enrolled in developmental courses. At first I thought these classes were a waste of time, but now I feel differently. After passing the developmental courses, I was determined more than ever to continue my education. Passing was the boost I needed for my ego. I realized how much I missed in high school because of my lack of interest to learn.

Now, I am interested in learning. In hopes of finding a major that will enable me to help others, I am attending college on a part-time schedule, trying to work my way up to being a full-time student. When asked my major, I tell people it is "Physical Therapy," even though after each day that I attend class and learn more, I want to change my major. One morning I read an article from *National Geographic* on "Eagles on the Rise" and when I was finished reading, I wanted to be a biologist. That same afternoon, after studying for my psychology test, I wanted to further my education in psychology. And that following night, after having written a paper for my English class, I was inspired towards another goal, studying and taking future courses in literature and creative writing. Going back to college has opened up a lot of avenues for me, and I am really grateful for this change towards open-mindedness.

I am concerned about the challenge that lies ahead in furthering my education. Even now, I am still a carpenter going through the motions. When times get hard and I do not want to be at my job, I tell myself, "Kate, get a better education and move on to a better job. This will take time, but in the end it will be worth all of this." Giving up a lot of things, such as buying clothes anytime I feel a need for something new, running the streets looking for that quick rush of excitement, and going places my friends go that require a dress code and a pocket full of money has been very hard. As I see it now, these things are no great loss. I have always been the laid-back, easy-going type person. Finding things to do without money has been most enjoyable.

Planting my feet firmly on the ground sometimes still becomes a hassle. Even now, with my new friends and a few of my old friends, I still manage to have a conflict about the way I am changing my life. Refusing to give in, I continue to believe I was not put on this earth to only please other people. Instead I was put here to live my life, to fulfill my ambitions and attain my contentment. Every chance I get, I am accepting the challenges of change head on. I find it hard to understand why other people want to hinder the improvement of my life. In my past experiences, I have done a lot of things that other people have not. I am not resentful about my past; instead, I use what I have learned, good and bad, to turn around and walk away from my past. The list of obstacles I have yet to face will go on forever. When I'm working for something I really believe in and feel good about, no matter what mishaps I might face, I know deep in my heart I can work through them. One day when I'm able to look back, all obstacles will seem trivial compared to what I will have accomplished!

Joy Lynn Fox

Going to college had never crossed my mind. My haven for seventeen years had been my home and my precious children. Married at a very young age, I felt my place was at home being a mother and a loving support to my husband. We lived simply, but happily, and my husband was able to go on and graduate from college. I, on the other hand, felt fulfilled and complete in the role I had chosen. Having been a talented person growing up, I channelled all my qualities into my children. We read books, wrote poems, and played sports of all kinds. I tried to instill in them a love for all humanity and creation, and my husband and I kept them active in church. We had heartaches and tragedies like all families, but basically ours was a family of love and commitment to each other.

Over the years I had developed good relationships with my children, but as they entered their teen-age years I began to feel the natural chasm that typically develops between parent and child as they strive for independence. I was suddenly left with a void I could not explain. My life was changing, and I didn't like it one bit! I was no longer needed in the same ways that I had been. There was a strange sense of loneliness as I saw my children growing up and growing away. It took me a while, but I began to realize that my career of seventeen years was drastically changing. My life would never be the same again. At first it was enough to enjoy my children's accomplishments and to be "Mom's taxi," but my heart began speaking something else to me. Its words were terrifying, yet so challenging that I couldn't get them out of my mind. My heart's desire was telling me that I had more to do and more to give in this life, and now for the first time I had the opportunity. I felt that an education would be the only way to get on the path to a new life.

My world had been so safe and sheltered; I had only worked briefly before the children were born. My mind reeled with all the handicaps I had. I felt totally estranged from the outside world as far as business and the educational system. Being in my thirties, I was worried about failure. What if I made one of the biggest decisions in my life and I couldn't make it? The sheer terror of it all kept me immobilized for a few months. Then one day I decided just to get some information from the local community college. After all, a little information couldn't hurt, and I probably wasn't eligible anyway. The catalog I was given caused a rush of adrenalin through my body: it sounded like there was a chance for me! I proceeded with all the applications and took the entrance exam. When my scores came back, they showed that I would have to begin on a remedial and developmental level. At first I felt a little embarrassed at not having made the college level, but I knew in my heart the strength and courage it had taken for me to come this far. In short, I was very proud. My joy was brief, however, when I realized that the next step was to find out how we were going to pay for this luxury with a growing family and one income.

We held a family meeting and explained my dream to our children. They were very proud of me and even teased that I would be grounded if I didn't do my homework! We brainstormed for a while, and with a lot of give and take on everyone's side, we came up with a strict financial budget that would be a sacrifice to us all. Since teen-agers get more expensive as they get older, I felt a twang of guilt at having to ask them to sacrifice at this time in their lives. Part of my motivation for going to school was to make sure that they had a chance for an education, which would be difficult on one income. I decided to bury the guilt and accept the loving support from my family. Knowing that they believed in me was a great boost to my self-esteem.

With all papers signed, fees paid, books bought, and schedule complete, I anxiously awaited my first day of school. There were days when I wondered if I had lost my senses, and days when I felt I could leap tall buildings. On a good day, a word of admiration from a friend would puff me up like a cloud. Finally, however, my days of waiting were over. It was the night before my first day, and reality hit like an atom bomb. I tried to prepare everything early, setting out my clothes and books. As I went off to bed, I prayed for strength and stuck all my doubts and fears under my pillow.

The first day of school, the sun shone brightly, the birds were singing, and all seemed right with the world. I jumped in my car and enthusiastically began to drive the short distance to school. A strange thing happened, though, the closer I got to the school. The sun seemed to dim, the world felt scary, and I couldn't find the birds anywhere! With my heart pounding, I made it to the school, found a parking place, and began walking to my first class. I felt like a toddler being taken to nursery school for the first time. Fortunately, I had given myself ample time to locate the proper buildings and classrooms. In my insecurity, I felt like everyone I passed was staring at me. I also couldn't help but notice how young everyone was! As it turned out, I spied a couple of soul mates in their thirties in each class. It was a comfort to know I could share a common bond with them. In addition, as time went by, I made several good friends that were right out of high school. Even though I tried not to, I found myself throwing some motherly advice to them from time to time. "Don't forget about the test tomorrow," I would caution. They would nod obediently, just to humor me.

It took a couple of weeks for classes to get settled, and then we got down to the nitty-gritty. As homework began pouring in, and tests loomed on the horizon, I realized that my study skills were very poor and that it was going to be a challenge in itself to teach myself to study. I experimented with several tactics, trying to find out what would work for me. I started out in the bedroom with the door closed, but it seemed the phone was always ringing, so6meone was at the door, or it was my turn to drive the kids to gymnastics. I managed to get my work done, but I was not pleased with this frustrating situation. Later I tried going outside, thinking the solitude of the great outdoors would infuse me with great wisdom. I ended up chatting with a neighbor, petting the dogs or thinking that the yard needed to be mowed. Clearly, something had to change. As my workload increased, so did my frustration. Quite by accident, however, I found the solution to my problem. For some reason I woke up around 5:00 A.M. one morning and could not go back to sleep. I decided to get up and read for a few minutes, hoping that I would soon feel drowsy. The house was still and silent, and I felt a sense of total relaxation. I decided to skip the reading, made some coffee, and thought I would look over some school work that was due in a few days. Because I was a morning person anyway, my mind was keen and at its best. I spent the next two hours writing a paper for English class. There were no interruptions, just me, my paper and pen. From that morning on, I made those early hours my special time to study.

Having been a full-time homemaker for seventeen years, I was also faced with another problem that, to me, ran deeper than the ability to study. I had always been available for everyone at any time, and it was a source of great pleasure and joy for me to do so. One day my son was in a music concert at school, and all parents were invited. In fact, it was a special performance just for parents. I was saddened by the fact that he might be the only little boy there without his mom to cheer him on. Of course, my husband did the honors, which made me feel a little better.

I had made a point of always being home when my children got home from school, but now there were times when they came home to an empty house. It seemed like I was always turning down their requests for help and asking them to do more and more on their own. I began to see, however, that the pressure and guilt were coming from within myself, and I had to learn to let go of it for my sake and my children's. It was really neat to see my family in action in my absence. Meals were being prepared, clothes were being washed, and life in general was fairly normal. I was proud of their independence and accomplishments, and was able to let go and concentrate on my dream of going to college.

Although we had all agreed on the financial sacrifice, reality was another movie. I wondered if I had the heart to tell my daughter that she couldn't have a new dress for the school dance. My son was playing basketball, and had I not noticed that his feet had grown two inches? Saying "no" was hard, but we had good friends and family who were willing to loan dresses, shoes, and whatever else was needed. Taco Bell runs and Pizza Hut deliveries were sanctioned for special events. In reality, I don't think anyone really suffered at all.

In conclusion, I feel like I have really taken charge of my life. Even though I have just begun, I have already leaped over many hurdles that I thought I never could. I have set my sights on a nursing career and know that I have several years ahead of me before I see any fruit. Blossoms turn to fruit, and I feel like my life has many blossoms already. I also know that life will continue to get harder, as my children grow and prepare for college themselves. My goal is to be there for them in whatever capacity they need, but to also allow myself to have the gift of learning, and, ultimately, a career that will allow me to use my desire to help mankind, and the knowledge to carry it out.

Grant Berry

For me to be in college is highly improbable; that I am doing well in school teeters on the illogical. Considering my upbringing, past educational performance, and current responsibilities, one might say, "This guy hasn't got a chance." If I were a racehorse and college was the track, there would be few who would pick me to win, place, or show.

When I told my dad that I was going back to school, the only encouragement he offered was this: "Send me anywhere, but don't send me back to school." For my father school was the worst kind of prison, so I was raised believing that school at its best was a drag. My dad thought that the purpose of graduating from high school was so you never had to go back to school again, and I adopted this working stiff's philosophy.

I followed my dad's example like a man who double-crossed the mob follows a cement block to the bottom of the river. After graduation I went to work, plunging into the lukewarm waters of mediocrity. I was not raised to be a go-getter. All I was doing on my job bagging groceries was trading dollars for hours. I worked just hard enough to keep from getting fired, and I was paid just enough to keep from quitting. My dad has been a union factory worker for more than two decades, and he has never striven to be anything more than average. Nonetheless, he is a good man; I love him very much, and I respect him for being a responsible husband and father. He seldom, if ever, missed a day of work; he never left his paycheck at a bar, and none of our household appliances were ever carted off by a repo-man. He took his family to church each week, didn't light up or lift a glass, and he has celebrated his silver anniversary with his first, and only, wife. However, if he ever had a dream of being more than just a shop rat, I never knew about it.

On the other hand, my dreams were big, but my thoughts were small. I knew I wanted to go to work each day in a suit and tie; unfortunately, I could not define what it was I wanted to do. I told a few people that I wanted to have a job where I could dress suavely and carry a briefcase, and they laughed in my face. They said, "You'll never be anything," and I believed them. Even now I am envious of an immaculately dressed businessman. It is not the angry type of jealousy; it is the "wish it were me" variety.

Considering the way my father felt about school, college was a subject that seldom came up at our dinner table. I was not discouraged, nor was I encouraged to go to college; it was my choice. However, an eighteen-year-old boy with a job, car, and girlfriend, and a father who is outspoken about his hatred of school is not going to sit in a classroom if he doesn't have to. Besides, I thought I was already smarter than my parents.

Since I knew I was not going to further my education, and I didn't know what I wanted to do except wear a suit, high school was a disaster. I do not know how my teachers can respect themselves after passing me. In every high school there are cliques and classifications. I worked just hard enough to stay above the bottom, but I did not want to work hard enough to get into the clique with the honor roll students.

Even though I was raised in a good Christian home, the only things I cared about were partying and girls. I spent all of my minimum wage paycheck on beer, cigarettes, and young ladies. As a senior, I dated a girl who was twenty. She had no restrictions, and I tried to keep pace with her lifestyle. I would stay out drinking until 3:00 a.m. on school nights. The next morning I would sleep through class or just not show up. It became such a problem that the school sent letters to my parents telling them that I would not be joining my classmates for commencement if I didn't show up for class once in a while. This put the fear of the establishment in me because I knew the importance of graduating from high school. Nonetheless, I never once remember doing homework my senior year. Yet in June, they shook my hand and forked over a diploma as I smugly marched across the stage in a blue gown and square hat.

Since I felt I didn't deserve the piece of paper with the principal's and superintendent's signatures on it, I passed up not only a graduation party, but also a class ring and yearbook. If it were not for my diploma and senior pictures, there would not be enough evidence to convince a jury that I am guilty of attending high school at all. I did, however, celebrate with my friends on graduation night. I got loaded, misjudged a turn, flattened a stop sign, and got my car stuck. When I pushed my car with my girlfriend behind the steering wheel, mud from the spinning tire sprayed all over my nice clothes. It was quite a night, and looking back, it was quite a fitting closure for the end of high school.

I am twenty-seven years old now, and surprising as it may seem, this is a return trip to college. My first attempt at college was when I was nineteen. I had always dreamed of being a disc jockey, so I enrolled in a broadcasting class; however, my experience in college was as forgettable as high school. My habit of not doing homework carried over, and the class was such a yawner that I often forgot to attend. Miraculously, I managed to pull a C, but my dream was weak and quickly died. I did not enroll for the next term. My girlfriend, the one that kept me out late in high school, became pregnant with my child. We were married two days after my final class, which gave me another excuse not to continue my education.

So now I am back in school, but it's a different road I travel than when I was a teenager. Mom and Dad paid the amount in the right-hand column of my tuition bill then, but now I am determined to pay for college myself, even though I must miss the sound of the pizza delivery man's tires on my blacktop driveway. I hope to work my way out of my blue collar by paying for school with blue-collar cash.

As a meat-cutter, I usually spend between 45 and 50 hours a week with a knife in my hand. Some weeks I have spent 72 hours beneath a butcher's cap. In one two-week period I spent 141 hours with a bloody apron on, but in that time I managed to show up for all of my classes and get all of my homework done (except being short a few bibliography cards for my research paper).

Working full time and raising a family leaves me little free time. If I am not in class, I'm studying linking verbs or trying to figure out the difference between compound and complex sentences.

There are other obstacles and challenges staring me in the face. The tallest hurdle is a lack of time for meeting all my obligations. For instance, my wife works two nights a week, leaving me to care for my two daughters. A twelve-hour day at work can lead to an evening coma at home, so when Mom's punching little square buttons on a cash register, I hardly have the energy to pour corn flakes for my kids, let alone outline an argument-research paper.

Going to college means making choices, some of which bring criticism. My neighbors, for example, hate my sickly, brown lawn sandwiched between their lush, green, spotless plots of earth, which would be the envy of any football field. Just walking to my mailbox can be an awful reminder of how pitiful my lawn looks when I receive an unforgiving scowl from one of the groundskeepers who live on either side of me. It is embarrassing to have such a colorless lawn, but it will have to wait because I want more out of life than a half-acre of green turf. Right now my time and money are tied up in college courses instead of fertilizer and weed killer.

But the toughest obstacle is having to take away time from those I love most. I am proud of the relationship I have with my wife and kids, so it tears my guts out when I have to look into my daughter's sad face and explain that I can't go to the Christmas program she's been practicing for weeks because I have a final exam. It's not easy to tell my three-year-old that I can't push her on the swings because I have a cause-and-effect paper to write, or tell my seven-year-old that I can't build a snowman because I have a causal analysis essay to polish. As I tell my family that I can't go sledding with them, my wife lets out a big sigh, and my kids yell, "Pu-leeze Daddy, can't you come with us?" At these times I wonder if my dream of a college education can withstand such an emotional battering, or if it is even worth it. But I keep on keeping on because I must set a good example for the four little eyes that are keeping watch over their daddy's every move. I must succeed and pass on to them the right attitude toward school. This time when I graduate, because of the hurdles I've overcome, there will be a celebration—a proper one.

Leatrice Muniz

While thinking back on the challenges that I had to meet in getting to college, I am surprised that I am attending. It seems that when I start to plan to attend, I let someone or something get in my way.

When I was in my last year of high school, all I could think about was going to college and becoming a teacher. I always dreamed of being just like the teachers whom I called my heroes. As I filled out applications and visited different schools, my future began to take shape. I felt that I was ready for the challenge of being a college student. I knew just what I wanted to be and just how I was going to achieve my goal.

One afternoon, as I was trying on my cap and gown for my graduation, my mother came into my room. As she entered the room, her face was different. You see, if my mother was upset, she never showed it on her face; she was a professional at keeping her feelings hidden. But this time her face was drawn, like a child who was told she could not go out to play. She stood between me and the mirror and began to cry. As I looked at her, I felt a lump in my throat and quickly noticed a letter in her hand.

As we both stood there, I began to realize that I was not going to attend college. A feeling deep inside was not one of anger or hurt, just emptiness. I felt empty and still was not told what was in the letter my mother was holding.

Mom looked at me and said, "You can't go to college; the money is not available." With these words, these few words, I was struck down. I felt used by the people I called family. I wanted to leave home and never see my family again. But I stood back, as if I were getting ready to fight, and asked, "Why? Where is my money?"

My mother looked at me and tried to explain, but for some reason I really did not listen to her explanation. "The money you saved had to be used for an emergency," she said. "We have tried to replace it but have not been able to."

The entire time she talked to me, I just could not breathe. You see,

I worked for the money in that savings. I worked during the summer and after school and trusted my mother to hold on to it for my first year of college. While she explained the situation, I remembered I had applied for financial aid at the school I had planned on attending. But that was the letter in her hand. Because my family's income was a certain limit, it was too much for me to get aid.

After that, things were never the same. I blame my family for using my money, I blame my mother for not holding on to it, but above all, I blame myself for not taking charge of my life.

After graduation I gave up on going to college and received a job as a teaching assistant in a private school. I enjoyed working with the children and believed that this was the only way I could be able to teach. I looked forward to helping with each day's lessons and play groups. I felt satisfied and had gained respect from fellow workers in the school. Within a few months the teacher that I was assisting let me teach the class art. I had not felt so happy about anything I had done and soon found myself being recommended for other teaching jobs at other schools. I was amazed at what I had accomplished. After feeling like I was a failure for not attending college, my life started to feel like it was my own. And, taking charge of whatever happens to me was now in my hands.

After two years of working at the school, I was accepted at a local college. I had saved as much as possible and was offered a part-time position at the school I would attend. My life was back on track. A feeling of renewed hope and a willingness to forgive my family and myself was very clear. But that feeling of not being able to attend or finish school was still haunting me.

I had completed my first semester when my mother had a stroke. She was out with my father shopping at the mall and said she felt dizzy. She sat at a bench and passed out. The next thing that I remember was seeing her in the hospital. The woman who I remember being strong and very rarely seeing cry could not remember her own name. Even after all that had happened, I felt I needed to be there for my family. I chose to leave school and help take care of my mother. Since she was totally unable to take care of herself, I used the money I had saved to initially hire a nurse. I thought this was a good idea. In the morning the nurse would tend to my mother's needs, and when I returned home from work, I would be there for her. Things were never the same in my family life after the stroke. My father, who was much older than my mother, was also ill and was gradually getting worse. My sisters had their own families to worry about and were not always there to help. I began to feel like I was the parent. I was taking care of two people who I felt never needed to rely on anyone for help. I was drained of any hope of ever getting back to school. So I continued working and taking care of my parents. Once again my life was not my own, and I was not in charge.

Time went by very slowly. Winters were the worst time for me. I was trying to keep things happy during the holidays but was unsuccessful. Mother was in and out of the hospital, and Dad just stayed there after a while. I never felt cheated out of getting my education, though. They needed me, and I was going to be there until they did not need me any more.

Just a few weeks before Thanksgiving of 1986, my mother had another stroke. This one took her life. She was out of pain, I thought to myself, and was at peace. Once again I was empty. You see, I loved both my parents but was closer to Mother. This loss was one that I just cannot get over. Because my father was in the hospital, he could not attend Mother's funeral, and we were not able to tell him she passed away. One week after she passed away, my father took a turn for the worse. He had lung cancer. Years of smoking had caught up with him, and he slipped in and out of a coma. One evening just before Thanksgiving, my family was told he would not make it through the night. I sat there next to his bed, still thinking of how we never told him of Mother's passing, when Dad passed on. My life was torn in pieces. How could I go on without them in my life?

After a month of getting their affairs in order and moving to my own apartment, it was time I took back my life. I realize now that life is full of moral options; you can pick what will make you happy, or you can wait for your happiness and help others first. I chose to wait and finish my obligations to my family. I felt that being there when they needed me was fulfilling a promise I had once made to my mother. They took care of me, and I always had a roof over my head and clothes on my back. I remembered telling her that if she ever needed someone to take care of her, I wanted to be the one. I was back working as a teaching assistant again. It was like starting from the beginning and giving myself a second chance. I needed to penetrate a wall that had built up around me, take chances and fulfill my own dreams. I did not have much contact with the outside world. My family nicknamed me "Hermit" because I stayed in my home for long periods of time. I decided I would wait on trying to attend college, work and build a life of my own.

After a few months away from my family, I decided to return home to pick up some of my belongings when I noticed that two of my sisters were at the house. This to me was odd because they did not want to visit much after getting married. When I entered the house, they were standing in the living room. There were some objects that needed to be taken, and my sisters had gotten into a heated argument over them. They told me they wanted to sell the items that were left behind and split the money. I could not believe what I just heard. The items they wanted to sell were things that my parents had for years. To most people they did not mean much, but to me, it was a link to my own existence. I also noticed they wanted to sell things I had bought with the money I saved for school. The items were bought by myself for their use when they were still alive. I told them I wanted them back, but I was refused.

This was my last meeting with my sisters. Not only did I lose a great amount of money that I will never see again; I lost respect and trust for my family. I put the situation behind me and went on with my life. The time passed quickly since the last time I saw my family, and attending college was becoming an eluding mirage. There was an intense feeling of nothingness inside me. Everything existed, but nothing was real. When my parents were alive, they were instrumental in shaping a future outlook that I wanted to achieve. But, when they passed away, it was as if my dreams went with them. Even though my feelings of blaming my family for not being able to attend college were now a part of the past, I still blame myself.

I soon met someone who changed my life. His name is Daniel. I felt comfortable, and I am able to open up and confront feelings that I thought were gone when I lost my parents. His feelings about certain issues were the same as mine, and I feel close to him and safe. We both had dreams of attending college and were amazed at what kept us both from attending.

About seven months after meeting, we were married. I enjoyed being a wife and working full-time to help with household expenses. But as time passed, I wanted to go back to college. Going back to college was no longer a dream, but a challenge, and I was intent on this confrontation. I needed to take charge of my life. Daniel was excited. He wanted me to go and wanted to help in any way he could. He took out a loan to help me with my first year in school. I completed with satisfactory grades and was approved for a student loan for my next two semesters.

I still have an abundance of obstacles to hurdle. Money is still an issue. Working a full-time job can and does make it difficult to study. And my obligation to my husband is an important part of my life.

As I look back on the situations that prevented my returning to college, I believe now they happened for a reason. I may not have been ready to face the challenge of college. Maybe I needed a challenge in life to test my endurance and believe in myself. After all, wasn't it Hemingway who declared that "Man can be destroyed, but never defeated"? When I was finally called upon to take charge of my life, this was the perfect time to take action.

Michael Anthony Couch

There was never a doubt in my mind, growing up as a child, that I wouldn't be just like my dad. I just knew that I would graduate from high school, and the very next day, go to work with my dad for General Motors. My whole life was planned out for me. I'd have a good job, good pay, good benefits, and live happily every after. It's funny how some of the best made plans can go wrong. Before I even graduated, the plant that my dad worked for in Ohio closed, and he was transferred to the Marion General Motors plant in Indiana. The life that I had so carefully planned out for myself slowly but surely began to drift out of my reach. My working for General Motors after I graduated had always been such a "given" in my life that I'd never thought of my life in any other way. I never planned on college; after all, I had a job guaranteed and waiting for me at G.M., so why make things harder than they had to be on myself?

The fact is, I never really liked school anyway. I did fine up until the sixth grade. It was my sixth grade teacher, Mrs. Evans, that made me fear and learn to hate school. I was a shy, quiet kid that just happened to look like the class troublemaker. She mistook me for this other boy, and from then on out, branded me a troublemaker. Every day, while the other kids in my class were learning about the countries and customs of the world, she made me sit in a windowless storage room, all alone. I honestly believe that this nightmarish experience scarred me for the rest of my school years. It made me afraid of school, afraid to ask questions or to seek out help.

By the time I got to high school, I had managed to fool around enough to be given an ultimatum of either going to the local vocational school or being expelled. Rather than risk expulsion, I chose to attend the vocational school, although, looking back, I think I would have been better off with the expulsion. So my path was chosen. I would learn a trade at the vocational school, kill some time, and then graduate, and on to G.M. I had always been interested in how things worked, so I decided to become a mechanic.

I did well at the vocational school. Then, when my dad's plant closed and he was transferred, reality set in. The future that I had planned was gone. So with my plans shot, I decided to begin a career as a mechanic. While I was still in school, I worked part-time for a dealership. I worked hard, and did a good job, so upon graduation, I was hired full-time.

I was doing okay for myself working as a mechanic. I made decent money and could pay my rent. It wasn't too long after that when I met my wife, Lora. She was in the middle of her first year of college, and we fell in love. I believe that she was the one that instilled in me the belief that I could go to college and that I wasn't "stupid" like I had so long believed. I really never had anyone to push me or suggest to me to go to college, and let's face it, my school career wasn't so admirable. I guess I never really thought I could do it. Life was going well for us; I was working, and Lora continued with her studies. The more I got to know her, the more I wanted to be like her, in a sense, go to school, learn, and do something with my life. I just knew that someday I would.

In the summer of 1988, I had an accident at work. My friend had asked me to help him with a strut assembly. Something went wrong with the spring compressor, causing the strut spring to recoil upwards into my face. When it hit me, it lifted me up off the ground, plowing into my face with such a force that it ended up breaking my nose, fracturing my zygomatic bone that lies beneath and towards the outer part of the eye, and tearing into my right eye. I almost lost my eye in the accident. The doctors weren't even sure if I would regain full use of my eye until weeks after the bandages and stitches came out. It was a close call for me, and luckily, everything turned out okay, aside from some minor scars. Now, you might think me silly, or a bit crazy, but I believe that the accident, and the events that followed were almost like a message to me, telling me that this wasn't what God has in store for me. Before the accident, I had registered for school. Then when I got hurt, I had to back out.

Not long after the accident, there was a robbery at the shop where I worked. The only things taken were my tools; everyone else's were still in their toolboxes. I don't know if it was "divine intervention" or just plain old bad luck, but things just seemed to be out of my control. With my tools gone, I could no longer be a mechanic, so I went to work elsewhere. I found a job at a small plastics factory in Hamilton, Ohio, called Advanced Drainage Systems. I started out on production, helping to manufacture the drainage pipe. Although it was a good job, and I received various promotions, I still felt uneasy about it. I still had this feeling in my gut that there was something better out there for me.

In the spring of 1990, tragedy struck again. Lora's mother became very ill. Lora had come home from school and found her on the floor. At the hospital we found out that her mother had cancer that had metastasized from her lungs to her brain. We all knew that things were too far gone. Her mother, Alpha, was always good to me, and always made me feel good about myself, and now she was dying in front of our eyes, and we couldn't do a thing. We all knew that she didn't have long. It wasn't just the advanced cancer, but the chemotherapy and radiation that was quickly wearing her down. Lora and I pushed up our wedding plans, hoping that Alpha would live long enough to attend. The Friday before our wedding, she lapsed into a coma and never came out of it. It was one of the hardest things I have ever had to do, It was hard for Lora too, but we went on with our wedding. We knew that Alpha would not have wanted us to do anything else. She died August 6, 1990, one week after our wedding, and the day before Lora's birthday.

One month later, Lora's grandmother died, and then not long after her, Lora's uncle died. We were both always so lucky growing up, never having really to deal with such tragedies, and then it seems as though it all hit at once. Even now, almost three years later, we both still have trouble dealing with such heavy losses. But just like everything else, you take things in stride, both the good and bad, and you learn to live with them, and you move on. It took a while for things to get back on track. There are good days, and there are bad days.

Today, even with all the misfortune and tragedy that I have faced in my twenty-two years, I feel, in a strange way, that it has made me more loving of life: not just the "given" in life like parents and other loved ones, and nature, but of the things that are too often taken for granted, like a good education. I feel like now, for the first time in my life, I am beginning to get a grasp on things. I realize that there is nothing without an education. Nothing is secure these days. Gone are the days of old when a young person could walk in off the street and get a decent job at General Motors or any other big company. Today, in order to get anywhere, you have to make your own way. Things won't just happen; it is up to me to make my place in this world. I want to work hard for a future for me, my wife, and the family we hope to have someday. Hard work is the only way. It's being the best you can be and doing your best, whether that be in school or on the job. The only work worth doing is the kind that carries your sweat, your labor, and, most importantly, your dreams.

Here I am, starting from the bottom. My educational background is next to nothing, but I won't let that get me down. I know that I'll probably have to work harder and longer than others my age, but I also know that it will be worth it. I worked hard my first semester in college and was filled with pride when I saw the 3.33 G.P.A. on my final grades. Yes, there are so many paths that I have yet to travel, and so much more work and hardship that I have yet to endure, but this is my dream. As I see it, we are all given two choices in life. We either choose to succeed, and overcome our obstacles, or give in and stop trying. No matter how long it takes, or how much work I have to do, I will make my dream a reality.

Lacey Wray

Is bulimia a disease or just a habit? This question is frequently asked by people of all ages. Many people say that it's a disease, and others say that bulimia is just a bad habit that can be easily broken. I do not claim to know the appropriate answer, but I have some ideas from my own personal experience. My experience with bulimia began on January 6, 1988. I was 14 years old and a freshman in high school, but I had the self-confidence of a 5-year-old who was starting kindergarten.

During the previous September my father and now ex-step-mom invited me on a trip to North Carolina. I was extremely excited because my mom had only let me go on one other vacation with my father. When I went on the first vacation with my father, I was treated as a mere child, and I was not permitted to venture off and do things on my own. This time it was going to be different. A week at the beach, gorgeous guys—this was definitely a young teen's dream vacation. At least this was my dream vacation until my father totally destroyed it. My father and I were discussing our plans for the trip, and he made a comment that would impact my life forever. He very casually stated, as if he were only asking me what I would like for dinner, "I hope you lose some weight because I don't want to take a fat little girl with me to the beach!"

At that point I figured I'd lose the weight or I'd lose my chance for a dream vacation. I began a slow diet with an average weight loss of two pounds per week. I was happy, but my father just kept asking, "Aren't you going on a diet?" I began binging constantly because he upset me, and then so that I wouldn't gain the weight, I began the cycle of binging and purging, bulimia at its best. Many people feel that purging is difficult, but I found the task rather easy. In the beginning all that I needed to do was touch the back of my throat with two of my fingers, and I would begin vomiting. Eventually, I would eat and my body would automatically begin purging.

Before I knew it, I had lost 40 pounds in three months. I had successfully pleased my father and in the process pleased myself. Even though I stopped losing weight after the three months, I was still trapped in the cycle, and I couldn't escape. By the time we reached North Carolina, I had gone from a size 13-14 to a size 7-8. My skin had become extremely pale, and I was constantly tired. My hair had begun falling out, and my menstrual periods ceased.

It was at this point that I realized I had become extremely malnourished, and because of this I decided to start eating again. Within two months I had put on 60 pounds and felt as if I had betrayed my father. I decided to begin dieting again: this time the right way. I soon discovered it just isn't that easy to stop being bulimic. I felt as if the bulimia had taken over. Even though I tried to eat and not purge myself, it seemed as if my body was on automatic pilot. It was at this point that I admitted to myself, for the first time, that I had a disease.

For the past four years I have been on a diet roller-coaster. I would do fine for three or four days, and then I would willingly let the bulimia take over. Once I realized the bulimia had taken over, I would stop, but the cycle would soon start again. Gain weight, diet, bulimia, stop dieting, gain weight, etc. . . .

Well, finally for the first time since I began being bulimic, I have successfully escaped this self-destructive disease. I have been dieting, without letting the bulimia take over, since September 9, 1992. This may not seem to be an extremely long time to anyone else, but for me it seems like a lifetime. However, I constantly have the thought, "Go ahead; do it; it won't hurt you," in the back of my head. It may seem strange, but my disease has given me a greater understanding of alcohol and drug addiction. I truly can understand the need to "just do it." With the help of my understanding friend Brenda, I truly have the support I need. I am finally winning a battle I never thought would end.

Although I have friends whom I can talk to, I wish that I could be open with my mom and step-dad, but I am afraid they would feel as if it was their fault I have this problem or that they had raised me wrong. My father and I are no longer on speaking terms; I finally realized this wasn't the first incident in which he had made me feel insecure. However, I am still on speaking terms with my ex-step-mom. I recently told her what my father had said to me, and she became very angered by it. She was upset that I had not told her of this incident when it occurred, but she is still very supportive of me. Telling her of my problem was one of the first steps in my recovery.

I have one important message for others with this problem. Learn how to lean on your friends and family because sometimes a problem is too big to handle alone, and no one can expect you to have the strength of Superman. I always tried to succeed alone, but I now realize that sometimes a person has to ask for help in order to succeed.

If I had not asked for this help, I may not be alive today. I had always wanted to go to college, but in my time of sickness this did not matter to me. I am very glad for the chance I have been given to improve upon my education and my ways of life. It frightens me to think that an inner struggle, such as my inner struggle with bulimia, can destroy a person's chance for a future. I hope that with the education I am obtaining I can assist others to make a choice for life and a future, instead of the choice of self-destruction.

Rose Ann Snell

Getting an education is now the most important thing in my life. I am so sorry that I did not do this years ago. My life is half over, and I'm just now doing something about it. Fresh out of high school, I got married. James and I had a wonderful life with two baby boys. I thought my life was complete consisting of being a wife and mother. I was very happy in this environment. Sometimes life just isn't fair. My husband was killed, and I was left with two babies. Now that my children are mostly grown, "I must do something with my life!" Little did I know then that the amount of time, dedication, and money a college education requires can be overwhelming.

Joe, my youngest son, said to me one day, "Mom, why don't you go back to school?" I thought about it a while and decided that this is the only thing for me to do if I want to make a good living. I was so afraid to go back to school that I even had nightmares about it. After many anxiety attacks, I made the first phone call. After speaking to the adviser, I learned that I needed to take an entrance exam; the thought of it terrified me.

April 23, 1992, I entered the classroom with a pencil in hand as if I was a soldier prepared for war. I was so nervous that I could hear my heart beat. Three hours later, I was mortified at the results. I almost quit right then and there. The adviser assured me that indeed I was intelligent enough to attend college, but just rusty in my skills. I really felt inadequate; since my goal is nursing, people's lives are at stake, so I have to be somewhat intelligent. After that first test, I really felt doltish. I just knew that I wasn't bright enough for college courses, much less nursing. I love people and I want to help people, so I guess that is the drive that keeps pushing me onward. As I brushed a tear away from my eye, I said to myself, "I can't quit before I even get started. At least I have to try." Experts say, "The first step is the hardest," and thank God that is behind me now.

June 1, 1992, I entered the classroom. I chose summer school to get started because I thought that there wouldn't be many students; therefore, I wouldn't be so conspicuous. The night before my first day in school I couldn't sleep a wink, so my first impression on the teacher was a doozie. To make things worse, I walked in the classroom late. Now all eyes were upon me; I was so embarrassed, I could have died. I thought to myself, everybody is going to think I'm an old fool. My eyes were fixed, looking only straight ahead so I couldn't see anyone else in the classroom. Then the teacher smiled; the anxiety eased, and then I noticed that I was not the only old timer there. What a relief. I'm not alone.

Now that the initial embarrassment is over, I can finally learn something, and I did. Since most of my teachers are my age or younger, they don't intimidate me. Instead they are more like my friends, wanting to help me, which is a comforting feeling. The college kids all call me "Mom," and they seem glad I am here. I do love the kids in return. They are so carefree, full of energy, and so witty; just being around them makes me feel so young. Oh, how I love college; I look forward to it every day. It really is better the second time around.

My favorite class is English. Since I'm older, I have more things to write about. I do believe that I have lived an exciting life, and someday I would like to write about it; therefore, it will be to my advantage to comprehend writing skills. The first day in English class, when I sat down at the table, I saw a small TV set. I said to myself, "Oh, boy, are we going to watch TV in this class? School is certainly more fun than when I was in it years ago!" Much to my surprise, what I thought was a TV was a computer. Boy, did I feel foolish, but I had never seen a computer before. This new contraption scared me to death. Now I knew that I was sure to fail this class. Thank God, I had a wonderful teacher who walked us through the computer instructions step by step, and I was fortunate to have a neighbor classmate who was already familiar with computers, so altogether I finally learned how to operate the thing. Now I just love it; it's much better than a typewriter. The computer even tells you when you have misspelled a word; what a wonderful invention! I can't wait to use it now. It's so much fun; however, I feel somewhat guilty using it because it is almost like cheating.

Up until now I have written of the positive things of college, but there are many negative things as well. For me, the hardest thing to overcome is the time factor. Class time is no problem, but the homework is a killer. It's not that I don't want to do it, but the time it requires makes it somewhat impossible for me. This is where the kids have it over me. I have to run a household with expenses; therefore, I must work. I'm very fortunate to have employers that understand that I'm going back to college. I'm grateful for this. They encourage me every day to finish, knowing I will be leaving them in three years for my nursing career! I do hate to leave them, but waitressing isn't very rewarding. It's hard work with little pay and no future. Without my understanding employers and co-workers I would have been discouraged. Since my own parents are deceased and I am single, there isn't anybody at home to help and encourage me, so it is wonderful to have good friends. Between the job, the household, and college, there isn't any spare time at all. It seems my life is on hold for three years. There is no social life at all. Oh, how I would love to see a movie, or go shopping, or even watch T.V. I don't know what is going on in the world, because every spare minute my nose is in a book studying something. I knew it was going to be difficult, but I never knew to this degree. I just have to tell my friends "no," which is a little selfish, but I have my priorities. I want to be a good nurse. Everything else must come second. I have never been so dedicated as presently, because somehow I have lost 25 years; this is my last chance.

Besides the time factor, there are insufficient funds. I find it hard to even buy gasoline for my car, not to mention the shape it is in. I just hope and pray that my car doesn't break down, because I couldn't afford to repair it. Since I live in a rural area, I really need a car to go to college. The college I attend is a small community college that is 13 miles away from my home. I'm grateful that my college offers the courses I need for my degree, because I couldn't afford a university. Even though the college I attend is inexpensive compared to a university, I find it hard to afford my tuition and my books. Every spare dime is a gift from God, and I do believe He wants me to become a nurse and help others for Him. He has given me the will, so I know there must be a way; therefore, I am taking one day at a time.

Normal full-time nursing students will finish in two years; I will be grateful to finish in three years, due to the time that I can afford to give to my studies. I wish I could be so fortunate to attend college full time; however, I can only do so much. I am grateful God has blessed me with good health and the stamina to keep going. I really don't care how long it takes me to graduate. I can just see it now; my grown children in the audience at the graduation to honor Mom, "the graduate." I can't wait until that scene is reality.

Even if I was lucky enough to win the lottery and become a millionaire, I would still finish college and become a nurse. I'm not just attending college to get a better job, but to become a better person for myself and society. Yes, my attitude has changed greatly since that first dreadful day. The war is yet to be won, but I have certainly won the first battle. I still have to fight for the time and money. Aside from all this, I do have the dedication it takes, because I am a good soldier.

Carolyn Ann Street

My name is Carolyn Ann Skinner Street. I come from a family of five children, four boys and one girl. My parents were true believers in education, but my mother never finished school. My father did graduate from high school, and then went on to the army. He was the only one in his family who finished school. My father's parents did not go to school because they worked in the fields to help raise the other kids in their families. Education was not very important to his great-grandparents. I have always been pushed to get my education, so I went on to graduate from high school in 1978 in Seattle, Washington. At the age of eleven my mother and father separated, and we moved to Wellton, Arizona. There my mother was murdered right in front of me by her boyfriend. He shot her in the middle of the street on a sunny day. It was the year of 1971. I was 12 years old. That's when my whole world changed. I was no longer a young energetic child who loved everything about life, but a child who learned to hate and fear life. My family was no longer whole. We were torn apart. My brothers were sent to Texas, and I was sent back to Seattle, Washington to be raised by different relatives.

When you are not part of their family, things can be very difficult. So to make things easy, I raised myself the best I knew how at that age. I used what knowledge I was taught by my parents. I did not want to be a burden to those I was staying with. So I stayed out of the way most of the time. I spent a lot of the time by myself. I figured that if I kept to myself, it would relieve some of the tension.

At the age of sixteen I moved in with a relative who was on drugs. She was my aunt. That's when I learned all about drugs and how to use them. I started smoking marijuana first with my aunt and cousin. Then we graduated to rock cocaine. That was a whole new ball game for me. We started about five years ago in 1988. The high was totally different. Smoking this kind of drug was filled with excitement. I have never had a drug that can talk to you. It says things like "Let's stay up all night and get high" or "Let's buy more" or "Let's sail something out of the house" and so on. I couldn't imagine the thoughts that were going on in my head. I was very vulnerable at this time. I had no control of my self or knew who I was at that time. I was also raped by a so-called friend and beaten up by him; that's when I decided to take charge of myself and my life.

So one day I hid out for two weeks in Portland, Oregon in a shelter for abused women. I stayed there until I could get enough money saved up so I could take my two sons away from there. We moved to Casa Grand, Arizona. I thought by running away I could get my life together. I soon found out that if you don't face your problems, they will follow you, no matter where you go. When we arrived in Arizona, we had just a bag of clothes and no money. I applied at the Department of Economic Security for AFDC. I worked odd jobs to sustain myself and my two sons. During this time I started getting disgusted with myself and life again. I was starting to go into a deep depression. It was really starting to get next to me. So I started running around with the wrong crowd of people, and the drug scene was starting to pick up again. This time there was something different about myself. I was in control of what I was doing, and I could feel it deep down inside. The high was not the same. The excitement was no longer there. I was not the same person who lived in Portland, Oregon. Sure, I was depressed and un-happy about life, and I did not trust people, but I did not want to do drugs anymore. What I needed was something new in my life.

Just when I thought there was not anything for me in this life, I met James Street. We talked for a long time about life, and what my problem was, and what kind of life we both wanted. He was very under-standing about my situation and my feelings about people. He also let me know that he wanted to be with someone who was in control of her life. He would prefer to be with someone who did not use drugs or with someone who was willing to stop using them. He let me know that he would do all he could for me and be there for me when things got bad. He gave me a lot of support, and he did not buy me any drugs at all. He told me one day that if I wanted any kind of life, I was going to have to take charge of who I was. That made me do a lot of soul searching to find out who I was and what happened to me. What I found out is that I did not know who I was or what I wanted out of life.

I found out that I blamed myself for my mother's death, and the hatred I had for men all these years blinded me so much that I could not have any compassion or love for anybody. I did not know how to love. Those feelings were gone. I did not know that they were gone until I tried to care about James. I did not know my hatred for men was so strong. I liked him, but I was terrified of loving him, but he stuck by me through some horrible times. I stopped using drugs by myself; I did not go to a treatment center. By doing this I thought it would ease my depression. What I found out is that it intensified my withdrawals and cravings.

The dreams and the cravings were horrifying for me. I could see myself getting high. The smell of the cocaine was so very real. The high was so intense. I would wake up in a cold sweat shaking all over, and the cramps were so horrible that I thought my whole body was going to ball up in a knot. My stomach hurt so bad that I would ease out of bed so I would not wake up anybody. I would go into the bathroom and lock the door and stay there until I stopped shaking and the cramps stopped. When the cravings would start, it was like every part of my body wanted it. Sometimes I was afraid to go to sleep, but I was determined to fight this drug. It was not going to win. The first six months were very hard for me, but I had perseverance to stop using drugs.

I had a life out there, and I wanted to be a part of it. Yes, it was hard to stop using the drugs, but I had a lot of support from my husband and my children. It took a year for the dreams and cravings to stop bothering me, but I have overcome them. Now the challenge of my life is getting over my depression and the murder of my mother. I have been blaming myself for a long time about what happened. I felt like I could have stopped it. This is something I could not work out by myself, so I went to get help this time. I am learning to deal with my problem one day at a time and to deal with each emotion one at a time. One day I hope to be able to find peace with myself and to trust people again. I know I will be working on this problem for a long time, but I will overcome this problem too. During my discussion with my doctor, I made a decision to go to college and get a degree in accounting. I have always liked working on a computer and working with numbers. I don't get much money from AFDC, but I make every penny count. I would love to just go to school and not work, but I am the only support my family has right now. I don't mind working hard for what I want. I know that one day it will all work out for the best.

It has been five years since I have done drugs. My system never felt so good to be cleaned out of all those impurities. My mind is clear of evil thoughts, and my heart feels the beauty of the world, and not just the hurt and pain. What I have to look forward to is to graduate from school and to keep on seeing my doctor to get control of my depression.

I know that I do have the perseverance to keep on going. I am a strong-willed person who can control herself.

What I face in the long run is getting my degree and taking care of my children. One day, with a lot of work, I will be able to control my depression without the help of medication. One day I hope to be free of my fears.

Raynard C. Sousis

The house is quiet and peaceful, with my wife at work and my three children in bed asleep. I am overcome as I relax in my recliner surrounded by darkness; only the whispers from the stereo of sixties music break the silence in the room. The light from the street filters through my living room curtains breaking up the darkness, and the shadows from the light dancing on the wall in front of me place me into a hypnotic trance. Suddenly my trance is broken as the clock hanging on the wall chimes twelve. I look down at the cold bluish black steel of my thirty-eight revolver as I fumble it in my hands. I think to myself, "Is this all there is to life? How can God be so cruel?" As I contemplate suicide, I think back on my life experiences and conclude that my life is a complete failure.

I was able to cope with my life up until April, 1991. This is the time I received my discharge from the U.S. Air Force after serving seven and a half years. With my wife's help I decided to end my military career after receiving a job offer from my uncle to work in his New York business. The position of vice president of the company and a salary of forty thousand dollars a year to start sounded too good to pass up. When I arrived in New York at the end of April, 1991, my uncle informed me that business was slow and he could not hire me at that time. Well, I was not too worried because I had many talents and I was confident that I could find a good job somewhere. But unfortunately, after two weeks, I was unable to find anything in New York.

My wife and I chose to try the Atlanta, Georgia area since two of her sisters lived there and we would be able to stay with them for a while. I was able to find many jobs there, but none with enough income to support my family. After two weeks, we left for Nashville, Tennessee, because my wife's parents lived in Clarksville, which is only about fifty-five miles north of Nashville. After staying there a few weeks, we found that we liked the area and the people, and we decided to stay.

I tried my hand at being a salesman by working for two different car dealerships, which did not work out. Then I sold fire alarm systems door to door for a company named Vantronics. I could not get used to working for only commissions because I needed to bring in a weekly income to support my family. I finally went to work for Pizza Hut as a delivery driver. I worked many long hours and made very little money, but it was better than unemployment. My savings was completely exhausted; however, my wife finally got her nursing license transferred to Tennessee and was hired full time at a nearby hospital.

In August, 1991, I talked to the Unemployment Office about going to school to learn a professional trade. I found out that the state had an assistance program that paid for tuition in a two-year nursing degree program offered by Volunteer State College. I anxiously contacted the school and began my registration process. But my dream was shot down a few weeks later when I realized that my wife could not make enough money to support the family and pay the bills. Disappointed, I discontinued my pursuit and maintained my job at Pizza Hut.

Seven months later, after talking to a few real estate agents, I decided to attend a two-week school for real estate. I heard that real estate was doing well in Clarksville, so with my license in my hands, I affiliated with Coldwell Banker and moved from Nashville to Clarksville. The market was fair, but the competition was tough because there were too many agents and not enough customers. Unable to sell any houses, by June, 1992, I got out of the real estate business.

My wife was very disappointed in me and annoyed with my attitude. We began to argue about anything and everything, and it seemed that whatever I did, it was wrong. I began taking my anger and frustrations out on my children by constantly yelling at them for every little thing. One day my wife and I had a huge argument, and I packed up all of my clothes. As I started walking to the door, I heard laughter coming from the mouths of my children. They were actually glad that I was leaving! My heart was saddened as tears filled my eyes while I sat in the car. After a long talk with myself, I changed my mind and put my clothes back. As the days went by, things only got worse between my wife and me, and now, here I sit at the end of my rope.

As I raise the gun to my head, I look up and see an outline of a face breaking through the darkness in front of me. Impulsively, words of anger start to explode from inside of me as my mouth opens. But suddenly, the outline image becomes the face of my two-year-old son. I pause for a moment as I stare into his face and say to myself, "What am

I doing?" Without words, I understand every thought as I read his facial expressions. His head is tilted to one side, and his sleepy eyes look upwards at me as he wrinkles his eyebrows curiously as if to say, "What's wrong, Daddy?" Thoughts of my death force me to realize that my relief from life would have a devastating effect on my children and wife. Trying hard to fight back the tears rolling down my face, I reach out and embrace my son. His embrace of love and almost adult-like understanding sends chills up my spine as I think how close I came to leaving my family. At that moment I found the courage and determination to face and take control of my life.

The next morning, when my wife came home from work, I kept her up for several hours explaining my plans to go to college and get a degree. After a long debate, she agreed that this would be a smart thing to do. The next day I drove to Austin Peay State University to talk to a career counselor. She put me on a computer that helped me to determine both my strong points and the career choices that I would be best in. After several days of thinking, I decided to go for an engineering technology degree. I then went to talk to the financial aid department, where I filled out the paper work for grants and loans. Since I had not earned any money in the past four months, I was confident that my wife would be able to support the family on just her income. I felt relief knowing that I will not have to drop out of college due to financial problems again.

Being thirty-six years old, I am nervous about doing well in school since I have not attended in a long time. The university library is very helpful in getting me information about study techniques which will help me to get organized for my first semester classes. The college assessment test shows me what courses I must take to meet college level courses, and the staff also helps me sign up for them.

There will be many obstacles to overcome in the future, but I am not giving up. My wife's hospital has cut her work hours, forcing us to compensate for our monthly expenses by selling much of our personal belongings. We are filing for a Chapter 7 bankruptcy; hopefully, this will allow us to survive until I graduate.

I am preparing for my future now by getting involved with the organizations affiliated with my manufacturing technology degree. By meeting important people associated with the businesses in the area, I will enhance my chances for getting a good job after I graduate. I know that I must work hard on organizing my time to improve my chances for success, but I also need to spend some quality time with my family as well. This will be a challenge for me to maintain both my high grade point average and satisfy my family's needs. I intend to push myself in order to achieve my degree within the next four years. This will be a difficult goal to reach, because the developmental courses I must take put me behind in my goal about one year. I plan to attend as many summer courses as I can. But I must save the money to pay for these courses myself since my student loan amount only covers my books and tuition for the fall and the spring semesters.

Every day for me, as I attend college, is a learning experience, not only from the school work, but also about myself and my abilities. I feel more confident now than I have in a long time. Living now has opened up doors to many rewards simply because I have decided to take charge of my life.

Xinrong Liu

At my high school graduation, I received a card from my counselor. On it, there was a poem:

> Only as high as I reach can I grow;
> Only as deep as I look can I see;
> Only as much as I dream can I be.

I have always kept this poem on the first page of my notebook, and it has become an inspiration for me ever since. I was not raised in the United States. I came to this country when I was eighteen years old. My native language is Chinese, and I have been brought up with Chinese traditions. When I first landed at the Kansas City airport two years ago, I could only speak a few broken English words and did not have any clue of general conversation—I was absolutely lost.

For my first year in America, I was enrolled as a high school senior in Shenandoah, Iowa. After growing up in a city of nine million people, it was a big change for me to live in a rural town in southwest Iowa. Along with being unable to communicate, I had to face a completely different kind of culture. From food to teenagers' lifestyle, everything was new to me, and I needed to adjust to it all. My life was turned upside down, and I was totally confused.

Among all the problems, language was the biggest. Although I had been studying English at school, the American daily conversation was totally different from what I learned in the textbook. I could not understand the lecture in the classroom at all. In addition to speaking, reading was also difficult for me. I had to stop every few lines to look up words in the dictionary. Compared with other people, I spent twice as much time on school work. I gave up social activities to work on my language skills during weekends and vacations.

The extra amount of work was nothing compared with what I had to face emotionally. In China, I was a good student, and things had always come fairly easy for me. Now, I needed help everywhere. At

87

school, I tried everything to overcome my language disadvantage—talking to people, recording lectures, and borrowing notes. However, the progress seemed so slow that I felt I would never be able to get it. My grades dropped and so did my confidence. Many times I cried in bed at night and wondered why life was so rough on me. I wanted to give up and forget the whole deal. When these moments came, I would close my eyes, put the poem on my heart, and recite:

> Only as high as I reach can I grow;
> Only as deep as I look can I see;
> Only as much as I dream can I be.

Its magic inspiration and my determination of getting a higher education have amazingly kept me going.

On top of these problems, I have had to worry about my financial situation. Since it is impossible for me to get financial help from my family, I have decided to put myself through college. I knew it would be difficult, but I was willing to take the challenge because I treasure the value of education. With the help of several people and a couple of scholarships, I started at a community college. During the school year, I worked as an assistant for two professors and at a restaurant on weekends. My vacation time was spent in a factory as an assembly worker.

The road to college has not been easy for me. However, meeting all the challenges along the way has made me tougher and more experienced to face life's difficulties. Now that I have been in the United States for more than two years, the language and the culture are not problems for me any more. As a sophomore at Iowa Western Community College, I have been keeping a 4.0 GPA on a 4.0 scale. While being a member of the International Honor Society, my autobiography was published in the 15th edition of *The National Dean's List*. At school, I have been nominated as the most outstanding speech student and a two-term winner of an academic scholarship.

While being able to overcome my difficulties, I remember those people who are still having problems. I try to help them as I once was helped. Understanding their anxiety and emotional frustrations has led me to be a tutor in several courses. It is a real joy in my heart to see these students make progress.

My second year in college has been much better than the first. However, there is never an end to the challenges. Bettering my language skill is a continuing task, and school expenses are still my main concern. I have, however, learned to enjoy challenges. Trying my best and overcoming the difficulties have been true thrills in my life.

During this time, I have been trying to contribute my ability to the community. I give time to community services, help others whenever I can, and most importantly, promote understanding between China and America. I have been giving programs on China to various civic clubs and church organizations around the area. It is very important to me to see a good relationship between our two countries, for I love them both deeply.

I plan to get a B.S. degree in computer science and a secondary degree in international studies. Studying in graduate school is also part of the plan. A good education is one of many goals in my life. After finishing school, I would like to contribute my talent and ability to the society. With my bilingual and bicultural skills, I hope to work with international affairs. Some day, if my dream comes true, I would like to be an ambassador who devotes herself to promoting a better understanding and relationship between China and the United States.

This is only my second year in college, and I have a long way to go before achieving my goals. The battle with problems and difficulties will never stop as long as I keep setting higher goals. In order to reach the peak, I must have the confidence to overcome whatever is along the road. Through all the challenges, I have learned a lesson: determination and hard work make anything possible.

Deep in my heart, I will always believe in the poem:

> Only as high as I reach can I grow;
> Only as deep as I look can I see;
> Only as much as I dream can I be.

Sharon Conlin

From infancy to early teenage years, I grew up in Northampton, Massachusetts. My family lived on the second floor of a very old house on Olive Street. I basically grew up in poverty. My mother worked the graveyard shift at the Northampton State Hospital (and to this day is still there), and my father did not work. He was, and still is, an alcoholic and could not hold down a job. My childhood years were not very pleasant. Drinking made my father violent, and I was both a witness and a victim of abuse. As long as I can remember, I've had problems because of growing up in an alcoholic environment. To this day the smell of beer on my father's breath brings back many bad memories of our Olive Street apartment and my childhood there.

My sister Lisa and I grew up very close. She is ten months older than me. When she started kindergarten, I attended Head Start. I remember clearly the church on the corner of Main Street in the center of Northampton where the kids were dropped off by their parents. Inside the church there was a large room filled with rows of short tables with small chairs (perfect for children our size). Many shelves filled with books, crayons, paints, and brushes were placed against the walls. The walls were filled with doodles of art, which gave children pride in their work. But most of all I remember the jungle gym where I showed off when my mother and sister came to pick me up. I told my sister that it was okay for her to play on it, as if it were mine. The cold winter air would nip at my face as we walked out of the church together.

"Come on, Nelly," Lisa said as she patted the old Nova's car seat while the tires below were spinning on the frozen ground. Finally, we caught traction and pulled out on to the street.

"Mommy, do we have to go home?" I said, wishing there was somewhere else to go.

I remember dinner was always so quiet. We were afraid of saying something wrong. Although my father ate at the TV tray in the other room, we were afraid he would still hear us. After forcing ourselves to eat everything on our plates, we were allowed to watch some television before bedtime. My mother would usually tuck us in to bed at night, often being awakened by the sound of things being thrown in the other room. We could hear their voices shouting through the thin plaster walls.

"It's okay, Sharon. They will stop soon." Lisa spoke to me in a soft comforting voice until I fell back to sleep.

In the morning we would awake to my father sleeping on the couch. We would all be walking on thin ice, trying to be quiet as a mouse not to wake him.

My parents divorced when I was around nine years old. We were forced to move out of where we lived because the landlord sold the apartment. The people who bought the apartment were going to renovate, raising our rent so high my mother could no longer afford it. It was hard to believe we were actually leaving. I wish we could have left all the bad memories behind. My mother, sister and I moved into a rent-subsidized complex in another part of Northampton, called Meadow Brook Apartments. My mother continued to work at the Northampton State Hospital. She changed her hours, working 7:00 A.M. to 3:00 P.M., and left us with the responsibility to get ourselves to school, and it wasn't long before we sabotaged her trust. The school contacted our mother and informed her of our poor attendance.

We continued to rebel against her authority as well as the school's and ended up in Juvenile Court. The judge claimed that my mother was unfit and could not control us. Our family was separated temporarily until our lives were put in order. I ended up in a state program called Key, and my sister was sent to California to live with my uncle and aunt. I was back with my mother after about a month or two, but Lisa stayed in California for three years. Being an adolescent, I did not realize that I was not only hurting myself, but I was hurting my mother also. She was not an unfit mother. I was the unfit child. She was only trying to make our lives better than our past. I ended up taking advantage of her soft disposition and her kind heart.

After attending summer school and earning my way off the Key program, I was accepted in the Smith Vocational High School in Northampton. After experiencing the four required exploratory programs, my girlfriend Linda and I decided to enter the electrical field. Linda was my strength and helped me to succeed. She encouraged me to go to school and not to skip. I started doing better academically and earned my diploma through the electrical department.

Graduation day was finally here. On June 3rd, 1987, I can remember sitting in a large auditorium surrounded by my classmates waiting for my name to be called. The feeling of being up on stage receiving my diploma was wonderful. I looked around for the support of my mother and sister. When returning to my seat, I glanced at Linda with a smile.

My relationship with my father continued to get more distant as I grew older. I only saw him on special occasions, like his birthday and other holidays. I continued to be scared and intimidated by him by remembering the other side that most people don't see. However, I do believe inside my father is sorry about how he brought up his children. I know that he lives with the pain of never having control of his drinking and continues to live with the mistakes he has made in his life. I live with the patterns of behavior that are a result of the environment I grew up in with him. I am somewhat shy around people that I don't know, but very aggressive and the decision maker around the people that I'm close to. I try to always take a stand and avoid being like my mother, who never stood up to my father. I am very self-conscious and have low self-esteem. These behaviors left me determined not to live the way my mother had during my early childhood years, although, when I was nineteen, I found myself walking in the same path as my mother once did.

On February 29, 1989 I married Jim. We met through some people and had a great friendship for years and then eventually started dating and married three years later. I thought I knew Jim very well, but was blinded by love and did not see that his drinking would lead to the destruction of our marriage. We had a loving relationship in all other aspects, but I could not control his drinking. Eventually our whole relationship started deteriorating. There were many nights of fighting that made me feel as if I were a child again back in my bedroom on Olive Street. I realized I was a co-dependent like my mother was for so many years. I was relying on hope, like my mother did, that Jim would change.

I did a lot of reading about adult children of alcoholics and could relate to the many patterns of behavior I fell under. The readings talked about Al-Anon group meetings, and that is how I became familiar with them and even began to attend meetings.

"Welcome to Al-Anon," a women spoke in a warm, soft voice. She began the meeting with a reading of the twelve steps to recovery. My mind started to wander as I tried to relax and get comfortable on the gray fold-up chair. I began noticing all the different people seated around me in a circle. There were men and women of all different races and ages, ranging from about fourteen to fifty-five. By how they dressed, I assumed that some of them were from upper-class families, others from working middle-class and a majority low-income. However, we sat in that stuffy little room because we all had similar needs and knew that part of our lives were out of control, so we were there to help each other.

"Would you like to have a turn, Sharon?" the leader of the meeting asked as she read my name off the tag pinned to my shirt.

"Hi, my name is Sharon," I said.

"Hi," everyone responded in unison.

Being so lost in my feelings, I wasn't sure where to begin. My heart pounded and I started by saying, "My father is an alcoholic and I married an alcoholic. I'm here to try to understand myself. I'm always so irritable and continually try to take control over all situations. I'm a compulsive list maker," I said with a giggle, but felt like I was going to cry. "I hate when people drink a lot." My voice cracked and I felt a tear begin to roll down my face. I couldn't go on any further and ended with a "thanks."

As they continued around the circle, I realized that I was not alone and that others also felt insecure with their lives and had some of the same traits I do. I felt better just being there and learned a lot about myself. I used to think I was alone and now I knew that I was not.

The meeting ended with everyone standing and holding hands. The final words spoken in unison were, "Keep coming back—it works." I continued to go to Al-Anon meetings to try and find some answers for myself. Unfortunately, Jim did not want to receive any treatment, and our marriage ended in a divorce after about one year. To this day I do not blame Jim for our divorce. I know I was not perfect and had my own problems as well. I am glad to say we still remain friends.

After the divorce, I started working several meaningless jobs to support myself. I worked with disabled people Monday through Friday, waitressed a couple nights a week, and cooked on weekend mornings. Most of my time seemed to be spent at work, which was quite a change from being self-employed while I was married. Jim and I owned our own company, called L & J New Home Construction. We had sub-contracted people to build several homes during the years we were together and then sold them, which made our living conditions quite comfortable. When the real estate market boom died, we continued to spend our money as if it hadn't. Eventually, we found ourselves financially along with personally destroyed. We ended up losing our marriage and our business.

The divorce is what made me so determined to get my realtor's license. During my marriage, I had taken the required class hours and the state and general exam, but failed. Being in the position I was in after the divorce, I was hoping that passing the test would take me out of the unfulfilling jobs that I held. Disciplining myself to study harder for the test and working many hours left little time for any kind of social life.

Several months after the divorce, I felt the loss of closeness with my friends. It was partially because of my busy schedule, but mostly and more truly because I had changed. My free time no longer consisted of watching television or casually have a drink or two with friends. My friends' lack of interest in their own lives really began to turn me off. Most of my friends are single parents on welfare. They stopped caring about their appearance and self-esteem. They lived off the State's system and took advantage of everything they could, keeping educational goals and careers out of their mind. I did not stop caring for my friends or their children, but I was unable to continue to communicate with them on the same level. No longer could I express my feelings of happiness about my life, because I don't think they had the same happiness to share with me. Many of them were not motivated and had no focus on dreams or goals, like I did. The two people who were most supportive in my life, and always have been, were my mother and sister. They were my best friends, and we shared everything together. Linda and I still remain friends along with a few others. We share a lot of the same goals, and I enjoy being friends with these people who have a positive outlook on life.

Now a licensed real estate sales person, I have chosen to continue my education to meet a larger goal in life. To complete a Business Administration major will make the beginning of my future to become a top manager working for a real estate management firm.

If only I knew years ago what I know now. If only in high school I felt the inner pride of getting A's, as I know now in college. Back then, I don't recall the feeling of inner happiness as I do now with my life. I know now that I have taken a turn in the path that I was once on . . . and it is the right one.

Trena F. Brown

For the first time in my life, I felt life was going on without me. Somewhere, somehow I had lost control of my life, and I didn't have a clue to where I was heading. I was an unemployed mother, with a son who had just turned one year old. Recently, I had separated from his father, my husband of 11½ years. A feeling of despair had come over me; I wondered what would happen next.

Mom and Dad made provisions for my son and me to move in with them. My father was stricken with cancer, and I was more than happy to be there with him. Before coming home to Chicago, I lived in Germany, on an Army base. (My husband, David, was a supply sergeant there.) Mom and Dad had never seen their grandson, Damarr; surely the baby would cheer up my father and he'd be his humorous self again!

A few months had passed by, and my father's illness took a turn for the worse. He couldn't hold any food; his weight diminished to merely skin and bones. The ambulance came; red and white were the colors of the vehicle, but in my eyes, all I could see was black, as if a hearse was carrying him away. Daddy died a few days later on February 28, 1992, a day before my 32nd birthday. My father's love, kindness and sense of humor would be missed by us all; but I was glad that the suffering was over. A wave of relief had come over me, like a cool breeze on a hot summer day.

After Daddy's death, David and I grew further apart; we divorced a few months later. I was "free"! So why did I feel so destitute? Almost 12 years of marriage, gone. However, I have a beautiful son out of what once was a marriage, now a vacant lot.

During this time my mom and I grew closer. She had lost her husband of 30 years and I had lost mine of 12 years. We seemed to cling even more to my son, Damarr, especially Mom. Sometimes she would just hold him tight and never seemed to want to let go. Prayer and Damarr's presence have given us strength to look forward to the future and not dwell in the past. Life does move on after death and divorce.

Suddenly the future met me head on; I would take control of my life. For once I decided to do something for me, for the future. My thoughts were clarified. My first step was the unemployment office.

Searching through the want ads and the telephone book, I set up several interviews. Place after place, test after test, my gas gauge was on "E," and not one clerical or labor job for me. It was May, and I had been looking for a job since March and I hadn't found one yet!

My mom suggested going back to school. (Mom always felt it was essential to get a college education in this world to succeed.)

"How could I go to college? I'm broke, and besides I have been out of school for 12 years," I said to my mom.

Mom reminded me of the 4½ years I served in the Army. "Surely VA (Veterans' Administration) can help. Here's the number," Mother said.

"Okay, I'll call tomorrow."

The next morning I called the Veterans' office downtown. Two weeks later I received an application for a grant. I filled out the necessary forms and returned them, and in less than a month, I received the grant. I was delighted!

I decided to make an appointment with a counselor at South Suburban College in South Holland. The counselor told me I would have to take a placement test first. "Great," I thought, "another test!"

When I received the test results, I wasn't pleased at all. My math scores were terrible, and my other scores weren't so great either. At that very moment there were only two choices for me: give up entirely or work myself up from the bottom to the top. I chose the latter.

Instead of starting in the fall, I decided to take a summer class just to get the feel of going back to school. Math was the class I chose. My mom told me taking a math class in the summer was crazy! Mom had tried to once and had to drop the class due to the extensive study demands in such a short period of time. When she made that statement, I was determined more than ever to exceed.

General math was a six-week course. Mom watched my son while I went to school Monday through Thursday, 7:30 to 9:30 in the morning. After the first week of school, my mom got a job from 8:00 A.M. to 5:30 P.M. I couldn't believe it! I had three days to find a babysitter. I cried; questions overtook my thoughts. Who could I trust to watch my precious baby boy? Would I have to quit school?

Sister Susan and I attended the same church; I remembered her daughter had promised a few months earlier that she would watch

Damarr. I decided to call LaOra. She answered the phone. "LaOra, can you babysit for me Monday through Thursday from 7:30 to 9:30 A.M.?"

She said, "I work in the morning sometimes, but I'm sure I can get my schedule changed."

"That's okay, maybe I can find someone else." I said sadly. I heard Sister Susan in the background asking, "Is that Trena?"

She replied "Yes." LaOra explained to her mother my situation.

Susan graciously volunteered to babysit for me the whole summer. I told LaOra to tell her mom, "Thank you so much; praise the Lord!" My sadness immediately turned to joy.

The next five weeks were very strenuous; we covered two chapters a week, and on Mondays we turned in homework papers which were a fourth of an inch thick!

A week before the final exam, my teacher told me I was one point away from an "A." He explained to me in order for me to receive an "A," I must get an "A" on the final. In a way, I wished he had never told me that. The pressure was so thick, I could cut it and serve it as cheese with crackers. Over and over I told myself, "Just one more week, just one more week, then it'll be all over."

Finals were over, my headaches were gone, and the pressure had dissipated. It took over a month before I received my grade for the class, but it was worth the wait. Yes, yes, I received an "A." Glory be to God!

Fall is here; my classes are scheduled around my mom's schedule so she can watch Damarr. Mom works the night shift; she comes in at 9:30 in the morning, and I leave right out the door to make it to my English class at 10:00.

Going back to school is much harder than I imagined. I'm a full-time student attending classes Mondays, Wednesdays, and Fridays, so on Tuesdays and Thursdays I rise up early in the morning, before Damarr wakes up, to do my homework.

My son has so much energy; most of the time I have to wait until he takes a nap or retires for the evening before I can study or do home-work.

Damarr isn't quite two yet, but he's definitely in the terrible-two stage. Damarr challenges me just about every time I get a book out to study. During mid-terms one night, I was studying in bed for my math exam. My son laid his head on my math book, using the book as a pillow. In his own little way he was trying to get my attention.

"Pooh, get off Mommy's book. Honey, get off my book, please?"

He didn't budge. So I politely rolled him off my book. Damarr retaliated by snatching a page out of my $31.95 pre-algebra book! I couldn't believe it! Needless to say, I spanked his butt! But it didn't end there.

First Damarr flounced out of the bed. Then he went over to the dresser and picked up one of his favorite alphabet books and put it on top of my math book. He said, "Book, book, book, Mommy!"

Of course, this was Damarr's way of asking me to read to him now! He can be so demanding at times, but so loving also. At that time he had a sweet, innocent look upon his face; it was a look I would have loved to capture on film. It's funny how my anger calmed down to a gentle serenity, as if I were subject to his innocent big brown eyes. Closing my math book with the torn page inside, I embraced my son with all the love I could give him at the moment. Against the headboard I propped a few more pillows, and I read to my son *Words from A-Z*, not once but twice. We drifted off to sleep. The next morning I arose well rested and resumed studying for my math exam.

All in all, my dedication is paying off; I'm pulling in three A's and one B.

My academic goal is to receive a degree in Social Service, focusing foremost on single parents. I'm not going to let being a single parent overtake me; I will overturn this situation and help others by acquiring my degree. Experience is sometimes the best teacher, and I feel through my experience and dedication I can be an asset to the community and at the same time help others, which is a reward in itself.

This degree will take roughly four years. The way I figure, what's four years of my life for something I sincerely want? School will be over before I realize it, and I'll look back and understand it's because I took charge of my life and said, "I can do it!"

Marilyn Kent-Krigger

"There are three types of people," Mr. Merriweather, my junior high school guidance counselor, chanted to the class. "There are those who make things happen, there are those who watch things happen, and then there are those people who stand around wondering, 'What the heck happened?'" We all laughed at the humor of his simplistic classification, but after the laughter had subsided, I seriously asked myself, "Marilyn, what type are you?"

I was raised according to very strict fundamentalist Baptist principles, emphasizing that God is omnipotent; therefore, He knows everything one is going to do even before the thought is formed in one's mind. All of one's actions, even one's very thoughts, have been predestined before creation. As a teenager, I interpreted the predestination to mean that no mere human could, nor should attempt to change the course that had been divinely assigned to us. God knows what is best for His people and only an evil sinner would attempt to contradict Him; therefore, I did not claim to be one who "made things happen."

I have always had a passion for reading and researching, and since studying was so much fun for me, I excelled academically throughout high school. I couldn't understand why anyone would remain ignorant about anything when information was so easily attainable through books, news media, and the reminiscing of elders. I definitely did not count myself as one of those who stood around wondering what happened, because I prided myself in staying informed.

During my youth, I labeled myself as one of those who "watches things happen." Indeed, one of my favorite activities was to sit in Shawnee Park and watch folks drive or walk by. I would let my imagination flow as I made up stories to go with the people I saw. For example, upon seeing a young, curly-haired woman, wearing a bright orange halter top and matching hot pants, walking quickly down the walkway with her arms folded tightly up under her breasts, and frowning and puffing so severely that she appeared to be blowing up an invisible balloon, I would tell myself that she obviously rode to the park in a bright red sports car with a good-looking, smooth-talking, playboy named Maurice who got a little too fresh when he tried to kiss her, causing the young lady to slap his face, leave the car, and since she failed to heed her mother's warning to always carry cab fare, was forced to walk home from the park. Then I would look for someone else to build a new story around. I loved watching things happen, and throughout my teenage years, I believed that my watchful attitude worked for me.

Because of my academic achievements in high school, I entered college in 1974 with an accounting scholarship to Bellarmine College, a very prestigious, private college in Louisville, Kentucky, locally renowned for its high academic standards and its excellent accounting department. The honor and glory of being accepted to Bellarmine quickly faded as I discovered that college learning did not come as easily to me as high school studies. In fact, I had such a difficult time adjusting to college life that I lost my scholarship after my first semester because I failed to maintain the required 3.0 grade point average. As I watched my four-year scholarship fly out the window, I told myself, "Well, I guess God didn't want me to have that scholarship. He must want me to work my way through school so I will appreciate my degree." So I got a job working as a security guard at night and on the weekends, and I went to school during the day. I saw that I was having a hard time working full time and going to school full time, but I continued to struggle through until I graduated with a very unimpressive 2.3 grade point average.

After graduation, I married my childhood sweetheart, Tim. Tim had also graduated and was fortunate enough to land a well-paying job with Xerox, but in Ohio. We had to relocate, and I could clearly see that I was leaving a network of accounting connections that could have helped me in my career endeavors, but I was sure God had a plan for me in Ohio as a housewife.

I had visualized a life of happiness, love, and success in Ohio, but after about a year, disillusionment began to set in. The first thing that went wrong was job hunting. I had a college education, an accounting degree, my passport to a well-paying job; however, I could not even land a bookkeeping job. A lack of experience and a bad job market erased my dreams of being a successful accountant, so I decided to concentrate on being a happy homemaker. The second thing that went wrong was my marriage. I discovered that Tim was having an affair with an attractive and successful co-worker of his. When I confronted Tim with my findings, he did not deny the accusations but tried to explain to me that he was just going through a "second thought" phase that all men go through during the first year of marriage, and I was not to make too big a deal of it. "After all," Tim said in his own defense, "it's not like I'm beating you or anything. You've got a nice apartment to live in, and I'm here most of the time. Surely, you can put up with this one fault of mine. I put up with enough of your faults."

The very foundation that built my dreams and my beliefs on appeared to be crumbling right before my very eyes. "Why was God letting my life turn so sour?" I asked myself as my questions led to more questions. "What happened to the meaning of our wedding vows? What happened to the guarantee that a college degree would secure a well-paying job? What happened to God's divine plan for me?" I could not understand what was happening to my life.

In a desperate attempt to find out why God would place me in such a terrible situation, I became obsessed with studying the Bible and searching the Scriptures for answers. I joined a Bible study class, and for six months, I reevaluated my interpretation of predestination and my part in directing my life. In the Bible, I ran across Scriptures such as, "Faith without works is dead. (James 1:10)," and "Be doers of the word and not just hearers (James 1:22)." But the Biblical message that made the most impact on me was the parable of the three servants and their talents, found in the book of Matthew 25:14-30. According to this fable, a wealthy man had to leave his country for a while on business. The man had three servants, and he gave them each a certain amount of money to keep while he was gone. The master gave the first servant five talents (coins), the second servant two talents, and the third servant one talent. When the wealthy man returned, he found that the servant who was given five talents and the servant who was given two talents had invested what they were originally given and had doubled their money for the master. The master was so pleased with these two good and faithful servants that he praised them and told them they could keep the earnings for themselves. However, the servant who was originally given one talent had hid his coin while the master was away. The servant told the master that he did not invest his coin because he assumed the master wanted him to be satisfied with what he was given and if the master wanted him to have more, the master would have given him more. The master was furious. The master called the servant "lazy" and took away the servant's one talent and gave it to the servant who now had ten talents. Then the master banished the lazy servant into "darkness and constant anguish." I started to realize that I had been behaving like the lazy servant, and I had been making excuses to explain why I could not take control of my life.

During the next five years, I underwent a change. The change did not occur instantaneously, but evolved slowly, gradually, like a metamorphosis. All my life I had believed that God preferred His people to just let life happen. I still had trouble feeling comfortable with the idea that I could change my circumstances and still be in God's will, but I finally gathered up enough courage to make an initial step. I filed for divorce and joined the Army.

I entered the Army looking for a haven of security and stability. I entered the military trying to escape the chaos and unreliability of civilian life. But, while I was in the Army, I found myself doing things I never believed I could do before, and I was starting to realize that success was directly proportionate to the amount of effort employed. For example, during my first week in basic training, I was unable to do two pushups. By the end of a month, with repeated practice, I found myself doing 30 perfect pushups. Initially, I was unable to run across the street without getting winded, but within six weeks, I was capable of running two miles easily. While my accomplishments did not merit a space on the front page of the local newspaper, every developed skill, every completed task, every conquered handicap, gave me the ability, the desire, and the courage to zealously approach other challenges.

My time in the Army, along with my continued Bible study and resulting spiritual growth, transformed me from an apathetic victim of life into a very active participant in life. I left the Army more mentally and spiritually mature, with a multicolor personality and ready and eager to spread my wings. As I used to sit in Shawnee Park and seek out subjects to build little stories around, now I had the desire to seek out challenges to build plans of attack around.

After being discharged from the Army, I discovered that life in the military did not keep pace with the modern advantages of civilian life. "PC's" and "floppy disks" were parts of a business lingo with which I was not familiar, and since I was not familiar with the language, the use of such items was even more foreign to me. I had to familiarize myself with modern business tools and accounting principles. But I could not wait on a refresher course before I found some way to bring money in. I needed immediate employment. What a challenge!

I began tackling my challenge by praying to God for guidance. Prayer would get me in the proper, positive frame of mind. After I had prayed, I sat down, listed all my possible options for immediate employment, and mapped out a course of action. I decided that the best boss I could work for at the time would be myself. After all, I understood my situation better than anyone else could. So I decided to take in toddlers during the day. I took children from two years old to four years old. The money was good and regular, the work was challenging yet enjoyable, and my evenings were free to update my accounting knowledge. So I enrolled in Northlake Community College to take a few non-credit courses. I signed up for a personal computer class, a refresher business accounting class, and a speed reading class.

After a couple of semesters, I was ready to approach the accounting field again. As before, my first step was to pray to God for guidance; then I started my search. Like an obsessive gambler who is driven by the belief that the next chance will bring luck, I attacked the want ads, the Texas Employment Commission's microfiche, and the telephone book. Accounting clerk, accounts receivable, accounts payable, staff accountant, experienced required, no experience necessary, entry level, management level—I applied for any and all positions that required accounting abilities. I was determined not to let anything discourage me or turn me away from my goal.

I went to many interviews with no success. Then, one day, I received a phone call to an interview as a staff accountant for a retail catalog mail order service called Sportspages. I had a very optimistic feeling about the interview. I somehow knew that I would land the job. Well, I was right. Sportspages offered me the accounts payable supervisor's position. I had reached another goal. I had succeeded!

Could I rest now? Definitely, not! I needed another mountain to climb. I felt like I could have anything I wanted. Oh, but what was my heart's desire?

I was an accountant because I wanted to land a job that was connected to my accounting degree. I had an accounting degree only because I was offered an accounting scholarship in my youth, and even though I had lost my scholarship during the first semester of college, I did not use the initiative to pursue another field of interest. So, what career would I prefer?

When I was a child, I had wanted to grow up to be a nurse. I had originally planned to study nursing after I had graduated from high school. When I had received the accounting scholarship, I thought that the accounting field must have been my divinely chosen destiny. But now I had spiritually matured enough to know that I could choose which path I should follow, depending on where I wanted to go. So, at the age of 35, I decided to pursue a nursing career.

Over 15 years had passed since I last attended college for credit

courses. Once again my first step was to pray for the stamina, perseverance, and courage to obtain my goal. Then, I investigated my options. I
discovered that the community colleges offered a nursing associate degree program. Since there are several community colleges in my county
and the tuition is quite affordable, the community college was an answer to my prayers.

I was a bit apprehensive about returning to a classroom situation.
So I signed up for a few telecourses for the first two semesters so I
could adjust to studying at my own pace. I did outstandingly in the telecourses. I was so proud of myself. My next step was to overcome my
fear of a classroom environment. I figured the best way to get used to
the water was to just jump in, and that is what I did. I took Speech
Communication. I figured I would have no choice but to participate in
class. Well, I loved the classroom environment, and I developed quite
an eagerness to participate in class. I now possess the confidence to take
a telecourse for convenience or a classroom course for the personal in-
teraction. I know I will excel in either one.

The nursing program was designed to be completed in six semesters for a full-time student. The program will probably take me about
twelve semesters because I am going part time, but I am so excited and
enthusiastic about my endeavor because I am doing so well and I already
have three semesters behind me with a 3.8 grade point average. How
wonderful! I have got so far to go before I will be certified as a registered nurse, and I am looking forward to every inch of the journey. Who
knows what direction I'll take after I have reached my nursing goal?

Mr. Merriweather said there were three types of people. What type
am I? I am the type that makes things happen. I no longer sit around,
satisfied with the belief that my life's journey has been pre-mapped for
me. I know I can make a difference, and more importantly, I act on my
knowledge to enhance my life. I am the type who watches things happen. I love to admire other people's accomplishments as well as mine. I
still enjoy watching folks in the park on a lazy summer afternoon. I also
love watching sunsets, rainfall, and children playing. I am the type who
wonders what happened. I am constantly reviewing and re-evaluating
my positions and situations in life. I learn from my mistakes and grow
strong from my victories. I also try to evaluate other people's successes
and failures. There is no need for me to re-invent the wheel.

Mr. Merriweather, I have combined the qualities of your three
types of people to create a fourth type. The fourth type is more successful, more complete, more satisfied. The fourth type is me.

Sherry Johnston

"Let us also lay aside every encumbrance, which so easily entangles us, and let us run with endurance the race that is set before us." As we are instructed in the Bible, we must do away with those things that will keep us from our goals. A runner faces hurdles and must decide how to approach them in the proper way if he is to progress. The alternative is that he will be stopped in the middle of the course. Hindrances, hurdles, obstacles, whatever they are termed, can help us grow and even help us with other difficulties later on. There are hindrances that I had to overcome to be where I am today.

I have a learning disability. When I read something, part of it gets lost. The problem shows up more in mathematics and some in reading comprehension. I began having difficulties in grade school. I didn't understand the work and began falling behind. I was tested and placed in a self-contained learning disabilities class. I hated the whole thing; I felt I was treated differently. The kids asked questions like, "Why aren't you in our class anymore?" I made up excuses like "the classes were smaller" or "I don't know." How was I supposed to explain something that I didn't understand?

I still wasn't accepting that I had a learning disability. When it came to the work, I was still doing a poor job. I was unhappy and confused. I resisted the teachers and the program. By being so uptight and scared, I made my early days very frustrating. I was only in second grade. I thought that being there meant that I was stupid. It took me many years to learn that I wasn't stupid. I now understand that there isn't anything wrong with going slower than the rest.

Until my junior year in high school, I was still enrolled in the special education program. In my junior year, I was tested, and it was determined that I scored too high to stay in the program. I had learned to compensate by learning the correct math concepts and to then use a calculator for accuracy. For the difficulty in reading comprehension, I used different techniques such as reading aloud or having someone read the material to me. At the time that I was told that I no longer needed the program, I was scared. I had found a safe and comfortable place in the self-contained class. It seemed as though I had just gotten used to the program, and now I had to move again. I didn't want to be the person they made fun of anymore. My teacher took me aside and talked with me. She said, "Sherry, will you look how far you have come? You have accomplished so many things. Quit looking at the bad things that could happen, and look at what you can accomplish now." I saw this person really had faith in me. The end result, my doing really well when I was mainstreamed, was very positive. I really needed someone to give me that word of encouragement and a push.

Another hurdle that I had to face was that of low self-esteem. In grade school I was alone: I had few friends. I was shy and introverted. When I was put in the special education class, some of the kids from the regular class found out and teased me. I was already self-conscious because of my size. I was taller than some of my teachers. Now there was something else "weird" about me, or so I thought. I was teased, told I was stupid and that I would never amount to anything. I believed all of it and hated everything about myself. I felt that way until my junior year. It took an English teacher to help me see my self-worth. He stopped teaching long enough to become a friend. He said it didn't matter what people thought about me. He told me, "Sherry, I know that you are not stupid. Just don't listen to them. They don't really know what you are like. You have to learn that you don't have to depend on what other people say to create who you are." This helped me to see who I was regardless of what others said or thought. Now I knew differently.

Not being supported by those who should have done so was also an obstacle I had to overcome. I can remember counselors saying that because of my learning disabilities, I would be limited in what I could do in life. I might have to settle for this job or that job instead of the one that I really wanted. I can remember one particular person who always encouraged me, my mom. "You can do whatever you set your mind to. You may have to work harder but you can do it," she said. Her encouragement seemed to be drowned out by the "settle for this" of the counselors and teachers. I was told that it was doubtful that I would make it as an interpreter for the deaf. I was introduced to sign language in junior high. The teacher introduced a few signs and then stopped. My interest kept growing. My family bought me books. I took sign language classes at church camp. I began signing songs at church. I found that I had a talent and that this is what I wanted to do with my life. My counselor said, "Oh, no, you are too slow." Luckily, I have learned to ignore these kinds of comments and go with my heart. I am enrolled at Phoenix College and receiving A's in my Sign Language class. I have a long road ahead of me; however, I am determined to get my degree.

Distractions, when I am supposed to be studying, are a problem I have to deal with. I spend too much time on the phone. I intend to concentrate on my homework, but I find myself talking to friends or writing letters. It is hard for me to say, "No, I can't do this or go there. I have to study." My schoolwork often suffers because I procrastinate. When I study in my room, it is full of distractions. My phone, radio, tape player and our cat are there. I find myself daydreaming, answering the phone, listening to tapes or petting the cat. I am often disturbed by family members. My brother wants to know if any calls have come in for him. The cat wants in or out or to be petted. Mom wants help with the chores around the house. It is easy to see where all my time goes— not to studying. I am now letting the answering machine do its job. I put the cat out before I start to study. My homework is now done before everyone gets home from work.

Last summer I got a job as a grocery store carryout. I decided to continue to work after school began. The store management said that they would work with me around my school schedule. At first this worked really well. The paychecks were smaller than in the summer, but it still allowed me to do all the things I wanted to do. I live at home, so there aren't any bills that I have to pay. I wanted to work so that I could have some financial independence. My work hours began to increase even though I requested several times for them to be cut. I was going to work almost as soon as I got home from school. I would come home so tired that I could barely make it through an assignment. I began falling asleep in class or sleeping through my bus stops on the way home. It came down to a choice of either work or school. I quit my job: school has a higher priority for me. Quitting my job left me with the problem of no money. I had been able to go out with friends before, using my own money. I have had to go back to depending on my parents for financial help. I was accustomed to spending more money than what they are giving me, but I'm helping around the house to get more. Next semester I am receiving aid and also two scholarships. This will allow me the time to study as well as give me back some of my financial independence.

All of the hurdles that I had and may face in the future can either be stepping stones or stone walls. I know what is important to me— school. By maintaining a positive attitude, budgeting my money, setting aside study time and time for me, I will have jumped the hurdles and be ready to finish the course. The hurdles have strengthened me and made me more determined to face any new ones. I see them as obstacles to be overcome, not ones that will overcome me.

Irina Marjan

Sometimes in my life, I have felt like the world's orphan. I have been shuttled between two countries, yet I don't fully belong to either one. I speak their languages, but I sound "foreign" to the native speakers of both. I have had two sets of parents, yet neither set has really wanted or accepted me. I turned 18, and I just started attending college. Even if neither of my two sets of parents has truly helped me, I am finding that I have my own two feet, and I'm beginning to stand on them.

In the beginning, I didn't know who my parents were or where I belonged. I was born in Queens, New York, and shipped off at nine months to Belgrade, Yugoslavia. My parents had their own problems and couldn't take proper care of me.

I lived with my grandparents and aunt and uncle in Lokve, Yugoslavia. For a long time, I thought that my aunt and uncle were my parents, so when my mother came to see me, I ran away from her because I didn't know who she was. My foster parents had never told me that they were not my parents, much less who my parents were. They didn't like my mother, so they didn't say a word to help me to understand who this strange visitor was. My mother was upset because I didn't want to talk to her. One day, she caught me by my hair and made me listen. "You listen," said the woman," I'm your mother." After that, she brought me back to the U.S., where I stayed with my parents for a year but was sent back to Yugoslavia because they still didn't get along, and I wasn't welcome any more.

At the age of five, when it was time to start school in Yugoslavia, the children in kindergarten were rude. I only had one friend, and we used to cry together because no one liked us. We would run out the door as soon as the teacher went on her break. I would run home, and my grandfather would bring me back to school. It was the "highlight" of every school day. My schoolmates reminded me about this till I was in seventh grade.

If this was not enough, then there was the obstacle of learning to speak Serbian. The Serbian language was the official language of Yugoslavia even though there were many other languages spoken regionally. For example, the school I attended was the school for the children of Romanian-speaking people living in the area. All of my classes were in Romanian except for my Serbian language class. At that school, the only foreign language offered was French. I had to make a decision whether to stay in that school and learn French or transfer to a Serbian school which had more foreign languages, including English, which I wanted to learn. If I'd transferred, then I'd have had to take all my classes in Serbian, which I hated. What I already detested in my Serbian language class were the prescribed essays that I had to write, in particular the perennial favorite "Moja domovina"—"My country." This was ironic because it wasn't even my country!

There was a Serbian school near by, but the Serbians who attended it were arrogant and had snobbish attitudes toward non-Serbians who wanted to go to their school. Therefore, I decided to stay and learn French. I never did learn English.

In the summer of 1988, at 14, I came to the U.S. to visit my parents. At that point, there was nothing for me to go back to in Yugoslavia because I had gotten to be too much of a responsibility for my aunt and uncle since I'd entered puberty. But ultimately I didn't want to go back because I knew I would have to attend a high school where classes were taught entirely in Serbian.

At that moment, I decided that I ought to remain in the U.S. My father still wanted to send me back, but that's when I started taking charge of my life. I told him that I wanted to stay in the U.S. and make something out of my life. I decided that I would go to school here and reach high. I would graduate with a master's degree in business some day. And I would speak and write perfect English.

A dream and the realization of a dream may be separated by many years and many hurdles. One hurdle for me was graduating from high school. High school was hard. I had to learn English. I had to make new friends. I had to work to make money. In English my biggest problem was my accent. I will never forget my first oral report. It was a health class, and we had to do a report on drugs and alcohol. I listened to everyone's report, but no one listened to mine. The whole class was laughing instead of listening. I had a strong accent, and I was reading very fast because I was nervous. It was funny for my classmates, but for me it was one of the worst experiences in my life. I had to talk to people who didn't care what I had to say about drugs and alcohol. Also, these rude people were the very people that I had to become friends with. I cried every day because I was lonely and had no one to call a friend. I had an accent, and I was different than everyone else. Therefore, it was hard for them to accept me. As my English improved, they began to accept me. I could feel that my life was getting better. I did better in my classes and became friends with many people. Still, I was working from 4 to 8 P.M. I had to stay up till 2 A.M. to finish my school work; I had to learn English and do well in my classes in order to graduate.

On a much smaller scale, even when things were improving, they had a way of making me stumble. The silly matter of my hair almost held me back from going to college this fall. I had damaged my hair badly with chemical processes, and I couldn't do anything to fix it because it was far too damaged. It was mixed gray, yellow straw, and brown. I was scared because I lost a lot of hair when I brushed it. Handfuls of the tangled colors came out. I didn't know how I could start college with so little and such hair. Finally, I cut it all to the roots and bravely started college with a boy's crew cut. I was not going to let anything push me aside in my path to a degree.

Now that I'm here in an English-speaking college on this side of the Atlantic at last, I foresee a rough road financially, but at 18 and with my sense that I can grapple with hardship and come out on my feet, I think I can do it. I work 25 hours a week for $5 an hour and have scheduled a full college load. I don't play around with perms or hair color, but I do keep my eyes on the prize. I'm beginning to feel as American as my passport declares, and I'm told by my teachers that I'm a real student.

I guess I had to learn who I was, where I came from, where I belonged, what I wanted to do with my life, and where I would want to live it before I could start taking charge of it. Now at 18, I've started taking charge of my life, and I'm trying to make the best of it. I can look back and see the long road from the tears in my first grade class to the hopeful and expectant attitude I bring to college, and to the rest of my life.

Christopher D. Hanson

My name is Christopher David Hanson. I was born on the fourth of November, 1968. Even though I am twenty-four years old, I am but a freshman in college. What you are about to read is my story. It is the story of how I came to take charge of my life, and my eventual decision to work and put myself through college. The decision to take charge of my life evolved through a painful process of self-centeredness, apathy, confusion, discipline, and eventual goal-setting.

I was seventeen years of age when my mom and stepfather went through a divorce. Back then, I did not care much about anything but myself. I was a self-centered, egotistical person who had little respect for anybody's rights or feelings. I pretty much learned this attitude from my stepfather, a perfect model of egotism. At the time, my mom went to Texas Women's University in Denton, Texas. With having to deal with a divorce, going to school full-time, and having to be a full-time parent as well, some support from me would have helped. However, I did not have time for that because I was too involved with myself as well as my girlfriend. I was nowhere to be found when it came to help, love, and support for my family. However, Eric, my younger brother, helped out and gave my mom some support. I really didn't know what my problem was back then and to this day, I still don't know. All I know is that I should have been a more supportive and caring son than I was.

At that time, I was employed by a grocery story called Safeway Stores Inc. As time went by, our business began to decline, due to an increasingly competitive market. By the beginning of my fourth year with the company, it was imminent that the company was going to go out of business. I immediately started to look for another job, preferably with another grocery store chain since I had become familiar with grocery retail.

Meanwhile, my grades in school were dropping drastically. With having to work thirty-plus hours a week, I devoted very little time to studying. I really did not care about my grades. Additionally, I lacked the ambition and drive to improve them. I kept telling myself that I could make a living doing grocery retail and that I did not need to deal with high school or college. Needless to say, that turned out to be the wrong way of thinking.

In addition to my self-centered approach to life, I acquired an apathetic attitude also. When I graduated on May 27, 1988, from high school, I took the summer off and started spending large amounts of money on myself as well as my girlfriend. Pretty soon, my money supply was getting very low; in fact, I virtually had nothing left. I lived with my mom and brother in a duplex and was making minimum wage at a grocery store. Since I appeared to lack a sense of direction, my mom told me to give college a try. I just looked at her in amazement. She even said she would pay for the first semester. I said, "What the heck?" I started in the fall taking only two classes. I took a remedial reading class and an emergency medical technician class. My plan at that time was to become a certified Emergency Medical Technical (EMT), attend fire fighter rookie school, and become a fireman in my home town. I failed miserably at this attempt. Unfortunately, I still maintained an apathetic attitude about the ultimate direction of my life.

As time went by, I become bored with my "chosen profession" in grocery retail. I lived from paycheck to paycheck. Also, I did not save any money for car insurance, gasoline for my truck, groceries, utilities, or any other necessary things in life. I at least saw that I needed to change my attitude and lifestyle to something better . . . but to what?

One day while I was working at the grocery store, I happened to see a man in a military uniform walk by. I recalled how my dad had been in the Coast Guard for four years and how positively he had always talked about that experience. Fortunately for me, the guy in the uniform happened to be a naval reservist. I asked him about the military, and he suggested that I give him a call. He then gave me his number and left. I thought about it all day long. I did not bother calling the reservist back, but went ahead to talk with an Army recruiter. I talked with a female recruiter for about an hour, and she gave me a little practice test that would roughly determine where I stood as far as entering the service goes. The test looked rather simple, so I completed it in a minimum of time. That was a big mistake on my part. I ended up failing it miserably. The recruiter gave me a little study guide for the Armed Services Vocational Aptitude Battery (A.S.V.A.B.) and told me to come back a week later to re-take the test. I was so disappointed in

myself. I couldn't believe I failed such a simple test. I knew I had to try
to take charge of my life and do something to remedy the situation I
was getting myself into. I drove straight home that night and started to
study that guide in order to make a better grade.

A week later, I went back to the Army recruiter to take the practice
A.S.V.A.B. again. I looked for the female recruiter I had met the previous week, but she was nowhere to be found. So, with nothing else to do,
and still masked by confusion as well, I went next door to the Navy recruiter and talked with him for a while. He told me how much higher
the caliber of training was in the Navy versus the training in the Army.
He told me about the Navy's schools and how their schools and education would benefit me when I went back to civilian life. The Navy
recruiter gave me a list of schools that I would be eligible to attend, and
I chose Gunner's Mate. This job or "rating" involved using missiles and
rockets as well as guns and small ammunition. The whole military idea
sounded so great: a steady paycheck; three square meals a day; medical
and dental care; and a roof over my head. I enlisted.

On the 25th of May, 1988, I reported for duty up to the naval base
in Great Lakes, Illinois. It was the first day of my required forty-two
days in basic training, and it was by no means fun! After having to get
up at 4:30 in the morning for the first two weeks, I was ready to get out
of the Navy. I had a feeling that joining the Navy was a very big mistake. However, I had signed up for four years in the Navy, and I knew I
had to stick with it and finish my enlistment. My total confusion and
lack of purpose made me fail to realize that being a member of the military would be so difficult. Although I experienced difficulty, I was
determined to see this through. One thing that helped me through was
that at the end of my enlistment, I would be able to receive my
Montgomery G.I. Bill Benefits. What this program does is that it allots
a certain amount of money each month to students who have served in
the military and are now attending college.

Throughout this period of confusion, I acquired a sense of personal
discipline in the Navy. I never realized the importance of personal discipline until I joined the Navy. On July 22, 1988, I graduated from boot
camp with honors and went on to Gunner's Mate School. To my disappointment, the school did not measure up to my expectations. As I
proceeded through the school, I realized that this profession was actually not my choice. I wanted a change and I wanted it now. I was told
that the only way I could get out of being a gunner's mate was if I were
to fail the exams. So, without hesitation, I failed them. When I was

called into my instructor's office, he told me that I needed to go see a counselor to see about getting another school. I was extremely happy to hear what he had to say, for I was determined to get into another school.

The next day, I talked to the base counselor and discovered all the schools were booked. I asked if I could be reinstated with the school I was previously in and was told no. My only alternative was to go to sea, watch people do their jobs, and see which one I would be best suited for. Once again, my expectations I had for the Navy quickly vanished.

In January of 1989, I was sent to an aircraft carrier that was currently being overhauled in the naval shipyard in Philadelphia, Pennsylvania. I was assigned to a division called "Firewatch," which consisted of watching welders weld the ship and make sure no sparks caught any debris on fire. I started thinking to myself that it could not get any worse than this.

One day when I had a day off, I had a talk with a friend of mine who was getting ready to be honorably discharged from the service. He was pretty high up in rank, and I asked why he wanted to get out of the service if he made good money. He told me that his options were better on the "outside" and that he planned to go to college, get a degree, and start a whole new life over again. Talking with him that day about his goals gave me a lot to think about in terms of *my* goals. Suddenly, a new perspective on life began to develop within me. I wanted to get out of the Navy and go to college. The urge to go to college grew so strong within me that I felt willing to do almost anything to get out of the Navy so that I could go.

However, I eventually came to understand that I had no choice but to come to terms with the fact that I had committed myself to a four-year enlistment in the Navy; therefore, I would have to serve my term and acquire a greater knowledge of discipline. The more I thought about it, the more I decided that since this was a four-year commitment of my life, I had better make the most of it. If I were to go Absent Without Leave (AWOL), it would have made things a lot worse. So I began to turn my negative attitude around to a more positive one. I started making many friends, which made survival that much easier. I also began to formulate a post-Navy plan which included college, getting a car, and getting a computer. In two and a half years, I managed to save roughly $14,700, quite a feat for somebody who likes to spend as much money as I do. But the big thing was that I had finally, after four *long* years, taken charge of my life. I had made a plan and set some personal goals. I could visualize myself going to college, making good grades, and actually working for something that had personal meaning to it. I had a goal in life—something I had never had before. I think the one major thing that I learned from my four years in the Navy is that in order for a person to improve his/her situation in life, achieving a higher education often becomes the first step. I hope to help young people establish a sense of direction in their lives and hopefully avoid some of the delays I took.

In conclusion, my journey to taking charge of my life evolved through a painful process of self-centeredness, apathy, confusion and discipline, to eventual goal-setting. I now face the future with anticipation and assurance that I will serve a meaningful purpose, and that I will hopefully make a significant impact on the future.

Lynn Macklin

I am writing this today not for myself, but rather for my father.

Let me tell you our family history, as I learned it at the knee of my grandmother. My father and mother met in the autumn, as the weather began to turn cold. They first laid eyes on each other at the local bowling alley, where the young people went to keep warm. A stray dog was roaming the parking lot with Ohio tags around its neck. My parents joined in the search to find the owners of this dog that had come so far. As they sat holding the dog on a dike that was built during the Great Depression to keep the flood waters out and to provide jobs to keep men together, they began to talk, to discover common interests and to form a bond. He was in eighth grade, she in seventh.

Thus would begin a love they dreamed would last a lifetime. They began to date each other, to the exclusion of all others.

When my mother was entering her senior year of high school, they discovered that I had been conceived. Their love for each other seemed to grow with the news; with sad but supportive parents, they carried on.

My mother stayed in school, delivered me in February, and graduated in June. My father, knowing he now had a baby on the way, joined the United States Navy as a way of providing for his impending family.

He would tell me later the tale of how, when he was training, he met a young man from the South whom he had befriended. This young man had joined the Navy to travel and see the world. When it came time to go meet with their placement counselor to decide where they would be stationed, each, in turn, relayed their wish list: my father to be near his not-yet wife, for you see they had yet to marry, who was with child; the young man from the South to be on a large ship that sailed the world. To this day my father laughs when he says the orders must have been mixed, for when they were posted, the young man from the South was on a tugboat that never left New York City, and my father was stationed on the *U.S.S. Guam*, which was always on the move.

After completing his training, my father came home and laid eyes on me for the first time. I was three weeks old. My parents were married while my father was home on leave in a quiet ceremony in my grandparents' home with me looking on. My father then left us to stay with my grandparents while he returned to complete his term of service.

My father finished his time, including one tour as a support person in the last group in Vietnam. He returned home and began work as a night janitor in the local hospital. When they cut back, he went to work raking leaves at a local park.

Our family, which had been on a waiting list, had been living with my grandparents. When our number came up for a spot in the local housing project, we moved in. It was here that our lives began to change. My father, using his G.I. Bill, began to attend the local college. This was the upside; the downside was that our housing complex, built to shelter returning veterans of World War Two, once a place of green grass and flowers, was beginning to show signs of wear and neglect. My mother too began to slip into a long deep depression.

As my mother's depression deepened, she became sullen; the woman I loved was slipping away just like the buildings around me. She no longer allowed my friends to come over to play. She began to go out to bars at night, coming home only to fall asleep on the couch, where she would become enraged if we made any noise.

One day, when I was seven, she did not come home at all. She had not said goodbye; she had just left us!

I watched over the years, as I grew, my father hold up the best he could. For this was the woman he loved. He worked during the day, kept the house, and went to school at night. He has never said a bad word about my mother. But I know he cries, late at night, when he's lying in his bed with his door closed. I would hear him cry softly, not in anger, in longing, in longing for my mother.

Much like the projects around us, my relationship with my mother began to slip away, I never heard from her, not on my birthday, not on Christmas, not on dark, cold nights when I needed her to bring light into me.

My father has done the best he could in raising a little girl all alone, like the little boy who put his finger in the dam to try and keep the water back. He finished college and found a job as a social worker. We hope to soon be able to move out of the apartment here in the projects I grew up in, which are still on the downward fall; crime, drugs, bathrooms falling apart, lives falling apart.

My present: I work part-time, as I have since I entered high school.

I try the best I can in school to make my dad proud. My future: I will someday have my teaching certificate, with which I will use computers to help children attain their highest reading levels possible. I firmly believe that it is through reading that we unlock a child's potential and allow that child a chance to succeed.

After you read all of the essays, if there is someone who needs help more, please do not hesitate to give it to them. For I will always have the strength my father has passed on to me. I will get by. I will find that light within me.

Thank you for taking the time to read my essay.

Ronald R. D'Avignon

Everything that happens to everybody every minute of every day helps to shape every aspect of their very beings; in addition, there are those who believe our personalities begin to develop even before we are conceived. I am one of those people who believe in genetic memory, that is, the transfer of strong emotional memories from parent to child via the genetic codes used to construct our bodies. This is the most logical explanation for the fact that I have developed a personality which so closely resembles that of the father I never knew. This is either the theoretical product of an in-depth contemplation of the facts available, or the best damn excuse I ever came up with to explain why I wasted thirty-six years of my life waiting for someone to drop a money bag stuffed full of one-hundred-dollar bills in my lap.

From the moment I was born, my mother tells me, I had a perfectionist's attitude just like my father. To hear her tell it, I was a perfect baby. I never cried, ate what was served me, never made a mess, and probably changed my own diapers. She said when I was learning to walk, she would catch me practicing in my bedroom when I thought I was alone, but nobody ever saw me walk until one day I got up and began confidently strolling through the house. Because they weren't expecting it, I almost escaped via the front door before they caught me. According to her, when I started walking, it was a perfect walk, never a stumble, never a stagger, just a perfect stride. When I was learning to talk, I never made a sound. Everybody would parrot at me and watch me mouthing the words, but never a peep was heard until one day I opened my mouth and began speaking in complete sentences. To this day I am afraid to do things I've never done before in front of others without benefit of private practice time to develop some semblance of proficiency.

As I grew up, my mother became afraid that I would develop a maladjusted emotional foundation because of the lack of a male role model; consequently, she began taking me to psychologists for evaluations. I didn't mind really; the tests were fun and the results were somewhat of an ego boost. According to the psychologists, I had an above-average IQ and the emotional development of a thirty-five-year-old man. While other children were worried about what kind of ice cream they were going to get at the store, I was worried about thermonuclear war. I would sit in my room for hours drawing maps of possible attack strategies and making plans for survival tactics in the event of attack. I cried myself to sleep at night worrying about losing my mother, my grandmother, and even my dog. The positive side of this is that I was always prepared to deal with any emergency, both physically and mentally. Having a high IQ was only partly beneficial. While I did find it easy to learn things that interested me, I found it extremely difficult to concentrate on things that did not. I have always been cursed with a very vivid imagination and am consequently subject to drifting off into daydreams when I'm bored. These three things, combined with a stubborn streak that would make a mule cringe, were the foundations for a very bad attitude toward educational, political, legal, and social systems.

During the time in which I was scheduled to start kindergarten, the common belief amongst new parents was that the average parent did not have sufficient qualifications to teach their own children, and therefore the responsibility of teaching children should be left to professionals. Because of this, when I asked my mother to teach me to read, she told me I had to wait until I was old enough to go to school. I had three books back then, three books that I loved more then life itself. I also had very little patience, so as soon as she told me that, I went to my room, put on my best shirt and pants, slipped on my black patent leather penny loafers (the ones with the Indian head pennies in them), put on my bright red blazer, donned my black gangster hat with the little red feather in the hat band, picked up my books, and waited for school. I had a long wait because I was only four years old at the time. I didn't forget, though, and when the time came, I was frantic with anticipation.

Upon arriving home from school that first day, I declared in no uncertain terms that I would no longer have anything to do with school. They had not taught me how to read, so going to school was a waste of time. When asked how I intended to support myself, I responded by saying I would get a paper route. That incident caused me to develop the attitude that if they weren't going to teach me what I wanted to learn, then I wasn't going to learn what they wanted to teach me. To this day, if I don't want to learn something, no matter how hard I try, I can't learn it.

My first four years of school went pretty smoothly. We moved around a lot, so the other children didn't really have time to get to know me. I also had a bad case of the cutes back then, which usually made me the apple of my teacher's eye. The teachers assigned to my classes from kindergarten to third grade all thought I was adorable. They encouraged me to do my best. They praised me when I did a good job and consoled me when I didn't. I liked school back then and maintained good grades.

By the time I made it to the fourth grade, my life was over. We had bought a house and set up a stable lifestyle. The house was old, the neighborhood was old, the schools were old, and the teachers were old. Two people had died in that house, and from the moment we moved in, I was hexed. My first day of school I came face to face with my worst nightmare. There standing in front of me was the epitome of disaster. My new teacher was the incarnation of the Wicked Witch of the West. She was mean, she was brutal, and she didn't think I was cute. She criticized me, she ridiculed me, and she failed me. I failed, and as far as I was concerned, that meant the effort was wasted. I have never been able to handle failure. I am a quitter, not a fighter. At that time in my life, I was convinced that if something was difficult to attain, then it wasn't worth having. That was the last time I even came close to putting any sort of effort into my school work, that is, until now.

From fourth grade on, I had nothing but trouble. I had lost my cuteness and replaced it was a large burly frame. The only socializing I encountered was when one of the bullies wanted to prove themselves bad by beating the hell out of me. The first time I was beaten by a teacher was in the fourth grade. I was standing in the hall when one of those bullies came up behind me and began beating me up again. I defended myself as best I could. When one of the teachers discovered us, instead of sending us to the principal's office, she sent us to the gym teacher, who promptly administered capital punishment on us both with a wooden baton. Since I was just defending myself, I thought the punishment without benefit of counsel was uncalled for. This was just the start. By the time I made it to ninth grade, I had been abused by four teachers and several dozen students. When I went to lunch, every day upon entering a table meant to seat some thirty-odd people would be emptied for me. I didn't go through one day where teachers and students alike didn't belittle me in front of my peers.

I started smoking in the ninth grade so I could hang around the other smokers and share cigarettes with my new friends. They all helped me smoke my cigarettes; however, instead of giving me friendship in return, they gave me mononucleosis. The mono soon turned to hepatitis, which was a blessing in disguise. I missed a year and a half of school because of that ailment, and when I returned, I made arrangements to double up on my eleventh and twelfth grades and get out of high school early.

These were just a few of the things that caused me to judge education in the manner in which I did. Since then I have taught myself carpentry, plumbing, banking, sales, and computer operations. The most important thing I've learned since I've been out of school, though, is that no matter how much technical knowledge you have, you won't get anywhere without a college degree, and that is why at thirty-six years old I am attempting to acquire my degree, even though to afford it I have to work forty hours a week and carry a full-time class schedule. With all this effort, I hope to at least be able to avoid joining the ranks of the homeless in my old age.

Gwendolyn Davis

In the past year, I have had to meet more challenges to get in college, stay in college, and continue going to college than I had to meet in my whole life. Looking back on my life, the challenges I have met have been for the sole purpose of me eventually attending college.

Growing up in a large family with my mother, father, five brothers, six sisters and myself gave me the feeling of security. I am the baby girl in my family. I felt blessed to obtain the special attention from my sisters, as well as my brothers.

At the age of four, I wanted so badly to attend school along with my sister and my two brothers Marshall and Tyrone. I was up at 6:00 in the morning to dress myself and to eat breakfast, with my coat in my arms ready to walk out the door with them. However, I was too young to attend school, so I had to wait until the following year.

The following year arrived, and I was registered for school. My sister Annie escorted me to my classroom. I began to cry; I felt frightened because I didn't know anyone. I thought my sister wasn't coming back to pick me up. However, I became relaxed and comfortable when I realized there would be other children my age that I could play with. I was enthused about coming home with homework to do like my older brothers and sisters. Every day as my sister did her homework, I was doing my homework. In a short period of time, I started recognizing my alphabets and numbers; my family was shocked. I received so much praise from all of them that it made me feel like a star.

I proceeded to excel in grade school. In the first and second grade, my test scores were 80 percent. In the third grade, I received several honor roll certificates. In the fourth, fifth, and sixth grade, I received achievement medals of excellence. I received a $50 savings bond as a reward for helping coordinate talent shows for my school.

I wanted very much to please my family, especially my mother. I wanted her to be proud of me. I was determined to excel in school. My sisters, brothers, and I did all we could as students, so my mother would realize that giving birth to all of us was not a burden, but a blessing.

My father was a heavy drinker and often abused my mother physically and mentally. My father's lack of concern to provide for the family emotionally and financially put a strain on my mother's life. Until this day we can see the strain in her physically and mentally.

In 1967, tragedies seemed to come in droves in my family's life. That year my baby brother was born with Down's syndrome, my parents separated, my oldest brother was drafted, two of my sisters got married, and three other sisters were sent to South Carolina to live. These changes would affect the rest of my life.

My mother, four brothers, one sister and I moved to a smaller apartment. I saw a change in all of us. My mother put her priorities in order; my brothers were expected to get after-school jobs; my sister and I were expected to help my mother with the daily chores. The stress that came with my father and a big family was gone; also gone, the family foundation. The changes my mother made helped salvage what was left of our family.

It was about this time that I was introduced to college by one of my sisters, who had recently started taking night classes at the community college near our new apartment. She would stop by on her way to classes about the time I would be sitting down to start my homework. She would talk to me about the courses she was taking and how I would one day be able to go, if I studied hard and kept getting good grades. I had my mind made up I would attend college as soon as I graduated from high school. However, I had to get through junior high school.

My first week in junior high school was exciting. Meeting different students with bad habits and attitudes got my full attention. I was surprised to see seventh and eighth graders smoking cigarettes, drinking alcohol, using drugs, and getting pregnant. I prayed to God that I never got weak during the challenges in this phase of my life and turn to self destruction. I tried to influence the ones I came in contact with hoping to change them in a positive direction. During our family discussions, my mother always gave us more than enough reasons why we should not smoke, drink alcohol, do drugs, or get pregnant. She explained the damage that it could do to us. I was very cautious not to get caught up in a bad situation. All around me I had seen teenagers involved in smoking, alcohol, drugs, and/or having babies, as my mother spoke about.

With all the extra responsibility that my mother put on me, I should have expected something bad to happen, and it did. I would not be getting promoted to the eighth grade because of my low reading level unless I sacrificed my summer to attend summer school. I realized I had to dedicate myself to my bedroom and not be with my friends or look at television. This was not an easy decision to make, but it was the best decision, so I could be placed in my right grade. I enjoyed staying home, reading novels, autobiographies, and short stories, and doing my homework for summer school. At the end of the summer, I received a 9.0 reading score. It was such a relief to know I would be getting promoted. The sacrifice was well worth it.

Disregarding my mother's sermons, at the age of 16, the one sister who still lived in the house with me became pregnant. This act made such an impact on my life. On April 8, 1977, Wanda gave birth to Latasha. Latasha brought joy into my life. I was hoping that this child would change Wanda for the better, but it made her worse. During Latasha's first week home, Wanda was nowhere to be found. This continued off and on for 18 months.

One day in particular, I was lying down taking a nap when Wanda came in my room and laid Latasha beside me. She said that she was going outside for an hour. Not two seconds later, Latasha began to regurgitate, and it smelled horrible, like feces. I called my brother. He kept an eye on Terry for me until I returned. I rushed Latasha to the hospital. The doctor immediately pumped her small stomach. Latasha was hospitalized for a week, and during that week we received results from the various tests that were given to her. The doctor informed us that Latasha had taken 15 one-a-day adult vitamins. He said that if she had fallen to sleep, she would not be here today. I could not stay calm; all I could do is cry. I thought this fatal accident would make Wanda more responsible. It did not affect her; she continued to choose her friends before her child.

My mother and I took the responsibility of raising Latasha. This brought another challenge to my life. When my mother had to meet her appointments for my baby brother, I had to stay home from school to be with Latasha.

One year later, I was faced with another challenge. I was now in the ninth grade, and my mother had to leave New York on an emergency because my grandmother was very ill. My mother left me with the responsibility of keeping the house in order. I was very mature for my age, and I knew I was able to follow instructions. During this emergency, I was home for two weeks from school for winter recess. I prepared my brother's meals, made sure that he was downstairs to meet the school bus on time, and made sure his clothes were prepared for the week. Wanda realized all that I had to do and volunteered my services to do her motherly duties. At the end of the first week of filling all these duties, I was exhausted. Even though I had taken on the responsibility of helping raise Latasha and Terry, I refused to let that stand in the way of receiving my diploma and going to college. In June of 1981, I graduated from William Howard Taft High School.

Graduating from high school in 1981 seemed like the opportune time to go to college. However, I also had a younger brother, a niece, and the moral obligation of helping my mother provide for them. Two years later, in 1983, these moral obligations were behind me.

I decided to move in with my boyfriend. Moving in with him brought unpleasant added living expenses and careless spending. In 1984, I gave birth to my daughter, Ashley, who is sincerely known as "The Pain"; she has been the most wonderful pleasant challenge. I was determined that life would be better for her and that I could not depend on my boyfriend for help. That first summer I couldn't find anyone in my family to babysit so I could take a typing course. I taught myself to type, working all day long so I could get a good job. I went ahead and did not stop. If I looked back, I was afraid I would never reach my goals. In 1987, I married my boyfriend, my daughter's father. That same year he joined the United States Army, and it changed our lives for the better. Our standard of living changed, and my opportunity to go to college seemed to be in sight.

It's now 1992, and my life is back to normal. It's the perfect time to go to college: My daughter is eight and very independent, my husband is very supportive, and I am very motivated. I realize now that all my challenges were a test to see if I had the drive and discipline to start and finish college. I have yet to start and not finish a single challenge that has come my way. It seems I have been waiting, waiting for someone or something to outright challenge me, to meet my goals.

On August 20, 1992, I received my challenge. A Pierce College bulletin came in the mail. I was reluctant at first to call, but I did because this seemed to be the perfect time to attend college. When I made the call, I was told to attend the orientation on the morning of the twenty-third of September. I started preparing myself for the orientation. I spoke to my supervisor to have the morning of the orientation off.

During the morning session of orientation, I was told that I had to take a placement test. I was also informed that preregistration had already taken place and no classes were still available. I became very upset because I felt that I should have been told about the placement test on August 20. At this point a part of me wanted to give up and forget about college, but I thought to myself that I didn't have any reason to go home.

My husband works full-time, my daughter is in school, and my mornings are free with nothing to do. I decided to take the placement test. After I received my score, I knew I had to take developmental courses in order to achieve an acceptable grade point average. I felt very eager and determined to better the grades that I had received from the placement test.

The first day of school never changes, whether it is kindergarten, twelfth grade, or college. The first day I was excited to be there, but felt a little apprehensive. I had been out of school for a long time, and I had a lot of hard work ahead of me. I thought back to when I did not have the opportunity to attend college, and now that I do, I have to face it head on. My very first class was math. It was exciting to learn math on a higher level. I was the type of person that never asked questions in class, but I understand now that asking questions is a big part of learning. Now I no longer just sit back and just observe; I get involved in class work and with other students. English was my second class, and I found it to be intriguing. I knew very little about using the English language properly, but now my vocabulary and writing skills have improved drastically. My third and final class was reading. With only three students and myself attending, I was able to get a lot of individual attention. I wasn't the best reader in the world, and I am still not, but I am learning more each week. The attention the teacher was able to give me shows. I read with more emphasis and better comprehension.

I enjoy college very much. It has given me a new confidence about myself. Unfortunately, it seems now I have come up against a challenge that may be harder than all my other challenges put together. The financial challenge that comes with attending college is more than I expected.

Writing this essay seems to be the means of conquering this challenge. To you I may be just another person who wants the opportunity to seek a higher education. Well, you are wrong; I am that person who needs an education. Everything that I am, everything that I want to be, depends on my getting a higher education. If I let this challenge stop me now, I may as well take away everything that makes me, because I see my future coming to a grinding halt, and it would take some time for my future to get back on track again. So I am hoping and praying that I am that lucky one who gets the opportunity to prove I am worthy, worthy enough to meet the challenges of a higher education. I cannot promise you anything in return for this chance to better myself, except society will benefit from this opportunity you are giving me, ten times over.

Josephine Thanhngoc Nguyen

Coming to the United States was one of the major assets that helped me get to college and my education. My strength and determination helped me overcome the obstacles that I faced before me. These major obstacles were getting accustomed to a new country, its culture, its language, and dealing with my family's financial problems.

Day by day, I sat on the porch in my motherland, Vietnam, feeling hopeless as if the world were going to end. As I sat there, the dream of getting an education and a career seemed infinitely out of reach. One day, while I was sitting on a rock at the beach, something hit me when I was looking out into the ocean. I realized there was hope for me if and only if I believed in my future. As I looked up into the endless blue sky, I could see my future out there waiting for me. It seemed to tell me to grab it in the palm of my hand. I then decided to set a goal for my future. Leaving my motherland and going to a country with freedom, the United States, was the very first thing I had to do. This meant that I had to leave my home, where I grew up for the last 12 years; my friends, whom I cared about and cherished; my relatives, whose love and care brought the family together; and finally my culture and customs, which I have always adored. The hardest thing was to leave everything behind and to start a new life.

In May, 1987, my dream finally came true. As I set my feet on the ground of America, I realized the opportunities that lay ahead of me. However, education was the only thing on my mind at that time. I then decided to take charge of my life and started my education which would lead to my future career. Having to struggle with many difficulties in learning the language and getting used to the culture and customs, I became the person who I am now proud to be.

My family, who have also been a very important part of my life, have brought me to where I am now. Even though my family has had the toughest time in the past few years arguing, fighting, and yelling, I still feel proud to have them in my life. My parents, who have always given me their love, care, trust, and understanding, have never once let me down, especially when it was the toughest and hardest times of my life. We have also had our ups and downs as any family would have, but somehow we have all learned to survive through them.

I remember, in the past, when my father used to pick me up at the middle school and bring me to many different places to help him out with translating English. It was a big help to him when he brought me to the insurance company, the housing authority, and the welfare office because he could not speak English yet. I tried my very best to understand the language, but it was only my first year here. My father, however, believed that I would make a difference and be a great help to the family.

I was also a great help to my family in other ways. They depended on me to answer the phone, to read the bills, and to cook for the family while my parents were out working. Furthermore, I was the one to go to the doctor with my grandparents as their translator. This was what I really disliked most because we sat there for several hours at the doctor's office. During this time I could have been studying. Because of this, I used to think that I did not have enough time to study and to get good grades in school. But as I grew up in the United States, I realized that these experiences helped me to grow and to mature. I also knew that my parents had always believed that I did well in school despite the fact that I helped out so much at home. I also became more independent and was happier that I was able to help other Vietnamese families adjust to their new places when they first arrived in the United States.

Cultural differences between Vietnam and the U.S.A. suddenly became my enemies. By the end of my junior year in high school, I remember explaining to my parents about my dreams. It was harder than anything that I had ever done. They didn't know that I planned to further my education. Unfortunately, my parents did not have any education when they grew up in Vietnam, and they felt they were too old to learn. Because of this, they did not understand how hard it was for me to get an education, especially when English was not my native language. They said to me, "Girls don't need to go to school and have a career; that's what boys are for." Furthermore, they added, "Girls are to stay home and take care of the house." I could not believe what I had heard! "This is me we're talking about. Mom! Dad! You are into old customs and are old-fashioned."

After several times of repeatedly trying to explain to them that we were not living in Vietnam, they finally came to their senses and realized how important my dream was to me. They finally supported me, but only under one circumstance, that I was to pay for my college education since they could not support me financially.

Having overcome these obstacles, I now have to face the reality of my financial problems when I go to college. Although I started working when I turned fourteen, the money that I had saved was not used for college. All the money was given to my parents since they could not support all five of us on their income. At that time, we were living on a day-to-day basis, which I wanted desperately to change. Since I was the oldest child in the family, I felt I needed to change this by getting an education and then a career.

At the end of my senior year, I was really lucky to have three small scholarships given to me for my excellent academics throughout high school. After high school, I decided to use my financial aid money and further my education at Middlesex County College.

Finally, I am almost overwhelmed by all the obstacles that I have yet to face at Middlesex County College. I am continuing my education here because I believe that my future is still out there, and all the opportunities are ahead of me. I want to enhance my knowledge, and Middlesex County College has the field that I am interested in. I always dream that someday I will become a medical laboratory technician. I am determined to get a bachelor's degree and further it with a career of my choice. Although I am in college now, I still have to face more obstacles on the way. Unfortunately, financial problems are still there for me to deal with. Right now I am still working at the same job I have had since I was fourteen, but I now work more hours. Sometimes I feel that I am on the road all alone since I cannot always depend on my family. On the other hand, I believe they still need me around to help out in any way I can. Because my family needs me, I decided to stay home and attend a college which is close by. As for me, I will always try my best to be there when they need me. I also know that my younger brothers will always need their older sister to help them with their school work. Because of these obstacles, I have tried my best to apply for scholarships during college. A little help will always make a difference in my future.

Lyndy Worsham

Every student struggles in her own, individual way; similarly, every student encounters obstacles throughout her life. Hardships are inevitable, but learning how to take charge of one's life is the crux of understanding how to survive and be successful. However, it is important to realize that each student comes from a different background where several factors may influence her performance in school, such as family problems, drugs, or a learning disability. No story of hardship will be the same. Here is my story.

Up until the age of ten, my life had been normal: television, school, slumber parties, and Oreo cookies (of course). Furthermore, I had a zealous interest in gymnastics: I would flip in, over, or on anything I saw. Then, in 1980, I went from my home in Texas to a world-famous gymnastics camp in Eugene, Oregon. Toward the end of the camp, one of the head coaches asked me if I would like to stay in Oregon (with my parents' consent) and be on his competitive team. The glamour I imagined and acceptance I felt were overwhelming. I was just a nobody from West Texas, but now I had the opportunity to make something of myself. After talking with the coaches and me, my parents reluctantly let their little girl go so that I could pursue my dream.

Needless to say, at the age of ten, I wasn't aware of what I was getting myself into. My schooling virtually stopped, which didn't concern me at the time; in retrospect, however, I can see that academic impediments were forming. We gymnasts were only schooled two to three hours a day; the remainder of our day—seven or eight hours—was spent in the gym. The training was rigorous. For me, the gym was no longer a place of laughter; it became a place of pain, tears, and broken dreams. Over a period of three years I clung tenaciously to my dream, but the vivacious little girl became obscured by disappointment and self-hating thoughts.

As the 1984 Olympic year came and went, I only watched on television with tears rolling down my dejected face while friends of mine performed and fulfilled their dreams. I was a failure in my eyes, too old for the next Olympics and becoming too womanly around the hips for elite competition. Thoughts of suicide reverberated throughout my mind. What did I have left (so I thought)? Then, in December of 1984, a spark of hope entered my mind, which was the torch that led me out of my miserably narrow world. I started to realize there was more to life than gymnastics. After pensive thought, I called my parents and told them I was coming home. They received me tenderly, to my surprise; after all, I was a failure, wasn't I? My mother hugged me, crying, as she said, "I'm glad my baby is home for good this time!"

After the excitement of home wore off, and after I had done just about everything my coaches never allowed me to do—dating, eating chocolate, or doing whatever a normal teenager would do—it was time to get back in school and be a regular kid for a change. However, I soon discovered most of my old friends had changed. There seemed to be an awkward emptiness to our conversations. I was different from most kids. I hadn't had the opportunity to grow academically or socially. My only friends had been gymnasts, and that was how my coaches wanted it. I wasn't far into my ninth grade year before I realized I hadn't learned much of what my peers already knew. I would ask them a question and hear a frequent reply, "You don't know how to do that?" To save the embarrassment, I rarely stopped my teachers even if I became totally lost. I hadn't learned the basics of math, such as fractions, decimals, or division. I had had no formal grammar course like most of the eighth grade students had. Needless to say, I was sinking fast.

My lack of schooling started showing in the classroom, and my teachers became concerned. After several conferences, my teachers and parents agreed that I should either be held back a grade or get a private tutor to catch me up on what I had missed and to help me understand the weekly assignments. Finally, we decided on a tutor, but the struggle did not end here. I had stepped into a totally unfamiliar world when I left the training center in Oregon, a world where I wasn't being told what to do, how to act, and what to eat. Suddenly, I was in school solving my own problems with a completely different focus and goal in mind: my focus had more room for creativity, and the goal was not so narrow and final. This is when I learned that the mind has no boundaries, and any limitations we feel we create ourselves.

My struggle became an internal battle in my head as well as an external battle with school work. Throughout high school I fought with a part of me that told me to quit, but I listened to my heart, which told me to endure the hardship. I learned not to be afraid to ask questions. I learned not to be afraid of what people thought. And most of all, I learned not to be afraid of failure as long as I got right back up there and learned from the mistake. The external battle was equally challenging: I worked twice as hard as the boy or girl next to me; I had to. I went to summer school while most of my friends went on vacation. Moreover, I was the first one in the math and writing tutor labs and the last one to leave. I endured the hardship and came out a winner! I graduated in 1989 in the top thirty percent of my class.

Through this hardship I set free a hunger for knowledge that could not end here. I am currently enrolled at Lane Community College, working my way through those same obstacles which hindered me through high school. However, I am removing these obstructions one by one. I am taking the basics again and realizing the importance of a strong academic foundation.

My principle is: if you don't know the basics, your learning will be obstructed by empty spaces. In addition to the basic English grammar course, I have taken a college vocabulary course, and I am enrolled in an advanced grammar course for next term. After taking the basic English grammar course in conjunction with the vocabulary course, I have immensely improved my confidence when I speak and write. I feel like a tuned violin. Furthermore, I realize how foolish it is to know big words but trip over simple pronoun-antecedent agreements. Finally, I am realizing the importance of communication and vocabulary; the more words I have to express myself means the more precisely I am able to communicate my thoughts to others. With each new word I learn comes a new angle of looking at my surroundings. Nevertheless, I must be careful to use the word appropriately and accurately.

My academic goal is to become an elementary school teacher. I believe the more I learn today means the more I can share with my students tomorrow. For me, being a part of a child's growth is so magical that every day is worthwhile. I realize the path I have chosen is not an easy one, and that I have so much more to learn; but I have the tools now to direct my life and take charge of my life. I intend on moving on to the University of Oregon next fall to work on a bachelor's degree in elementary education with a minor in special education. I will not give up on my dream because each time I try, I picture a child sitting next to me with the desire to read and me with the tool to give him or her that gift. What better service could this soul render?

Bernadete Piassa

My daughter is teaching me how to say "squirrel." My teacher is explaining to me the difference between "their" and "there." Although I am 38 years old and an award-winning journalist, I am struggling to learn these basic words because I am a foreigner. Seven years ago I moved from Brazil to the United States without speaking more than a few words of English. Now, I am attending college. But it wasn't easy for me to get where I am now.

I guess it all started when I was a child and lived in a small town in Brazil. I loved to collect postcards from distant places, and I would spend hours just looking at them while I imagined that I was traveling farther and farther from my hot and dusty town, where nothing seemed to happen. I would sit on the tile floor to cool myself off and spread all the postcards in front of me. Then, I would start my imaginary trip to Egypt, Greece, Japan, or somewhere else. Those days, I used to travel, truly, with my family. Sometimes we would take the boat and go to my uncle's farm, in the middle of the swamp. Other times, we would take the train and go to the south of Brazil, just for fun, or to Rio de Janeiro to visit my grandmother. But those trips weren't as interesting as the ones I made with my postcards, which would take me to wild and dangerous places.

Later on, I started to travel by myself in real life and went to Rio de Janeiro to study. It was there that I attended college for the first time. In order to get in, I needed to take a one-year preparatory class. That was a year of discoveries, hard work and fun. I had to work hard because it was very difficult to get a place in a public college in Brazil. These colleges were supposed to be the best ones, and since one didn't need to pay tuition, the competition was strong.

But I didn't need to study all day. There was still time to go to the beach with my friends and to discuss with them the political situation of Brazil. My friends and I were against the military government that ruled our country at that time. We had long discussions at the beach and at school about freedom of the press and about the future of Brazil.

At the preparatory school, there was a teacher of history that taught me a lot about the past of Brazil, showing me that my country hadn't always been in the mess it seemed to be those days. He enriched my life with valuable information, and with his help and the help of other teachers, I was able to get a place in the best college in Rio de Janeiro.

I started college there but ended up moving to Sao Paulo because it was easier to find a job as a journalist over there. In fact, it wasn't so easy to find the first job, but once I got it, I moved very fast to better positions, until I became an editor of women's magazines for the best publisher of Brazil. At that time I was already married with two children. But I hadn't forgotten the postcards of my childhood, or my dreams of traveling to distant places. So, when my husband was offered a job in New York, I was eager to go. No, I hadn't forgotten the postcards of my childhood; I had just forgotten that I would need to speak another language once I got to America.

In New York, I discovered soon that I was absolutely unable to communicate with anyone. The shock of this discovery was unbearable to me. I was used to being considered a smart person, a sophisticated writer, a skillful journalist, and now I was nobody. I couldn't read, write, or even watch TV.

I remember once when my husband invited some of his American friends over for dinner. They tried to talk to me, but soon realized that I couldn't understand. Therefore, I was condemned to spend the whole night just listening to them and smiling foolishly while I felt like crying. My head ached, my hands shook; I had never felt so diminished in my life. For long months I felt like that. In order to survive, and in order to endure the fear, I built a shell around myself. I wouldn't work, because I was too scared to talk to anyone. I was too scared to make even a small move.

The books helped me and my children, too. Although I was afraid, I still wanted the best for them. I started to go to the library and get children's books. I learned English reading "The Three Little Pigs" and looking up in the dictionary words like "wolf," "honey," and "friend." Afterwards, when I knew a little bit more and my children had gotten bigger, I read "The Magic School Bus" and looked in the dictionary for more complicated words like "waterfall," "sewer," and purification." Finally, I felt brave enough to try adults' books. I started with Agatha Christie's mysteries and searched in the dictionary for words like "suspect," "perseverance," and "mankind." Later, I moved to Amy Tan, Doris Lessing, and other contemporary authors. Although they were difficult for me, I was glad to realize that I was able to understand them.

Since I felt more comfortable with the English language, I started to dream of going to college and of learning how to write in English. But not until this year did I have the opportunity to take a test and get a place at Bucks County Community College. This time, my preparation for college was very different from the one I had in Brazil. Here, I could go to a preparatory class, or spend one whole year thinking about my future and the future of my country. The preparation I had was by myself, reading books. The school I had was the school of life.

Now that I am attending college again, it has been very strange to be back to school after all these years. I look at the other students in my class and remember the dreams I had when I was in college the first time. Like the other students, I had a lot of time to waste then; I also had a lot of dreams. What became of those dreams? They changed, for sure. I don't get my postcards out anymore and travel with them to distant places. I want to write, in English, about my distant country, about other emigrants who also came from distant countries and are not capable of telling the stories of the beautiful places they left behind.

I've seen articles written by emigrants' children telling how hard it was to grow up in a house where the parents spoke a different language, or how hard it was to see their parents getting scared and smaller once they were in the streets. But I haven't seen the emigrants telling their own stories because they don't know English well enough to write them. I would like to be the emigrants' voice. I would like to express their feelings: to show how strange it is to live in a country with different values, and how strange it is to dream every night of a country that belongs in your past.

I know that it is not going to be easy to tell these stories in English, but I hope one day I will make it. My daughter is teaching me how to say "squirrel." My teacher is explaining to me the difference between "their" and "there." Life already taught me to be patient and to believe strongly in my dreams.

Ruth Norris

Wash the dishes! Clean your room! Mow the grass! Phooey! When I grow up, I'm going to run my own life. Isn't that what all children say? Starting at around the age of ten, my goal was to live my own life my own way. By the age of seventeen I was married. I had freedom at last.

Just when everything seemed to be going my way, I realized that the love of my life was secretly a Nazi dictator who took his schooling on the right-hand side of Hitler. At least that's how it seemed to me. As if that wasn't enough, I learned the cold hard facts of divorce and the humiliation of having to move back in with my parents.

At the age of twenty-one, Mr. Stork brought me a bouncing baby boy. It only took me about a week to figure out that a child is not something you can just leave in the toy box when you are done playing. Years went by as I watched my son grow and my paychecks shrink. I was alone and in charge of my life, and boy was I having fun.

The answer to all my problems came while I was watching a soap opera: every family needs a father figure. I was married again. Now I was raising two boys. Which one actually had the higher I.Q. never was documented. Unlike a child, I could leave a husband in his toy box and never go back to play. This put my seven-year-old and me back into the single parent group.

A person doesn't need much to be in this group: just sign up on welfare. Unfortunately, in this group, a person doesn't get much. While it seemed to be working for us, somehow I had completely lost what I had always wanted. Now the Department of Human Services was in charge of my life.

School had still not entered my mind. I guess I thought since I had a high-school diploma, from 1977, who needed more? Maybe I did. I found this out when it came time to help my ten-year-old with his math homework. I don't remember doing that kind of math when I was young. I'll just make him study harder; that way I won't look so stupid.

The next year or so I don't really have any memory of. I did try marriage number three, but that was a very short one. I ended up just settling back in front of the television and accepting my fate.

My fate seemed to be the knowledge of the street. This had many good points. It gave me the know-how to survive. Book knowledge, on the other hand, is a lot different; for this I needed school. While I was having a hard time money-wise, keeping my son dressed properly and school supplies replenished, the need for my education entered my mind but was just a faraway dream.

I sat and watched the world go by. Many of my friends were going back to school, but they had more money and time to waste than I did. All my time was needed to impress the welfare system with my lack of worldly possessions. That in itself was a full-time job, and I was good at it. This became my big accomplishment. I was in control now. It's funny how things look when I keep my eyes closed.

While sitting—my most perfected art—and watching television one night, I was dreaming of all the things I would not be able to get my son for his thirteenth birthday. Thirteen, he was no longer a baby. He was turning into a teenager before my eyes. It won't be long before he becomes a young adult. Then he becomes completely independent. Next, he'll move into an apartment of his own. Oh my God! Then he will fall in love, get married, and have children! I'm going to be a lonely, old, fat grandmother facing the rest of my life with nothing to fill the void! Wake up, Ruth! Take charge of your life before it's over!

Who said that? Is it really possible that there is a little voice inside my head that can scream loud enough to register on a Richter scale? I have read about it in children's books, and I had watched it happen on television, but now it was happening to me. My inner self was wanting to come out. Most of all, my inner self was wanting to learn, to grow, and to become something.

After another week or two, I decided to check into the possibility of furthering my education. What could it hurt? I'll send for a Pell grant form, and if I'm accepted, maybe I'll go.

The application is here. I thought surely they would have lost my address. No problem; I'll just fill it out and see what happens. What is all this? A person has to have a college degree to understand the forms. How will I ever make it through school if I can't make it through the forms? Boy, am I in trouble.

Well, that chore is done and over. The papers are in the mail. It's in the hands of the U.S. Post Office now. I'm glad I don't have to worry about it anymore.

I can't believe it. They accepted me! Don't panic. The next step is the Asset Test. The secretary has assured me that I cannot flunk. That's a relief. Great, what am I going to wear? How do school kids dress these days? I hope it's not like my son. What am I doing? I'm thirty-three years old. I'm too old for this! Calm down; it's just a test, not a fashion show.

Everything is going pretty well. I have made it through the first part of the test without much trouble. The only part left is the math portion. I'll do okay unless there are a lot of fractions. What is all this short hand-looking number stuff? This can't be math. I'm doomed!

Well, the results are in. I'm not as dumb as I thought. My worst hurdle is going to be math. All my scores made it almost to college level. I'll be starting my first math class with the other four-year-olds at Noah's Ark Preschool.

What a feeling there is inside me. I have a sense of accomplishment and a sense of worth. The hardest part is yet to come. The toughest obstacle of all, I have found, is fear. That one little four-letter word has such an impact on me. It covers such a large variety of areas: failure, fitting in, acceptance, peer pressure, and rejection.

What will it be like if I can't make the grade? How will I handle sitting next to students who are fifteen years my junior and not knowing as much as they do? How will I watch some people do their work with what seems like second nature, while I pull at my gray hairs trying to make the simplest things come into perspective? What will they think of me? These questions ran through my head a million times before I ever set one foot in my first classroom.

The first day is here. Sitting outside the school with all my new books, pencils, paper, and wearing the new outfit my mother had bought me, I almost had a change of mind. "Start the car and drive away," I told myself out loud. Instead, I opened the car door and walked into class.

This is great! I'm not the oldest person here. I'm not even the fattest! This is going to be all right. Even my clothes are up to date with my age group. I feel good.

Time out. Maybe this isn't so great. It averages out for every hour I spend in school, I have three hours of homework. Time is going to be an important factor for the first time in a lot of years. Maybe it is a good thing my son is now a self-maintaining individual. The days are long, and television is now a luxury. This is so different, but I think I'm going to make it.

Who made up these rules? Mid-term tests? I'm not ready! Just when everything is going smoothly, someone throws in another test! I hope they don't make a habit of this. Let me guess, this is what school is, right? Right.

I'm actually doing it. I'm changing my life. Although it will take me until I am sixty-five to get through my math courses, everything else is falling into place. I used to think I would be just another Roseanne Arnold, but since I have enrolled in school, I see myself more as a Murphy Brown. Journalism has aroused my attention since I now feel intelligent enough to read a newspaper. I have a lot to share with people, and journalism can be my tool. I ended my first semester with a 3.6 grade point average. Pretty darn good for a woman of thirty-four.

All in all I believe I have finally done it. I am now in charge of my life. The funny part is, it has been a lot easier than I thought it would be. What I was so afraid of I will probably never really know. My future is not forged in steel, but it looks brighter than it used to. It makes me think of the yellow brick road in *The Wizard of Oz*. Even with a well-laid path, there will still be flying monkeys or a wicked witch trying to stop me. But with the dream inside me now a reality, the future looks pretty good. What seems so ironic to me is now I tell my son to wash the dishes, clean his room, and mow the grass. I only hope and pray it doesn't take him thirty-four years to find what I have.

Lynda S. Kissior

My motivation to enter college was the realization of a need in me: to find and understand who I, Lynda Kissior, am. I have spent most of my forty-five years serving others and trying to meet their needs before considering my own. I do not think of myself as being altruistic; rather I believe I was someone who encountered despairing situations in other people's lives. I would have gladly allowed someone to step into these dilemmas and take charge, but there was no one else, and I had to help provide for others' needs first before my own. Had I not had the strong desire to learn, the financial problems, the family responsibilities, and the personal obstacles confronting me in my daily life would have bound me in ignorance forever.

The financial hurdles I have had to leap stem from my placement in the lower middle-income bracket, a large mortgage payment on a home, a child to finish raising and the choice between being classified as an above-average student or another dropout. In the coming year, they will be lifted even higher due to my loss of the Pell grant and all other governmental financial aid. While I was fortunate in obtaining financial assistance for my first two semesters, my eligibility will be terminated due to the decrease in my dependents. In order to maintain a decent grade point average, I had to quit my job in October of 1992. This produced a loss of one thousand dollars' income a month which my family was accustomed to having for the larger expenses as well as the small comforts of living. Now, when my teenager says to me, "Mom, I need," I remorsefully ask, "Hon, can it wait?" Debts are made to wait instead of payment being on time; beans with corn bread are substituted for the weekly rib-eye steak smothered in sautéed onions.

My family has always made me the center of their lives. My husband and I have three children and three grandchildren. We raised and provided ample support for my oldest daughter through college and two divorces. Our son has married and is now serving in the United States Marine Corps. The youngest daughter is in high school and remains at home. But whether they live at home or are stationed across the sea, no matter what their problems are or what the crisis is, Mom can and will usually fix everything. But lately, I have had to let them down; or have I? Instead of running to Mom, they are having to learn to fend for themselves because I refuse to live only for them anymore. Sometimes my house is left to go unclean, for I have to choose between homework or dusting. I stay up late and long past the time of when my husband has arrived home from work and retired for the night. On occasion, my family has had to endure my shortness of time and patience where I have allowed frustration and exhaustion to build up in me because of stress from trying and eventually conquering a concept that was new to me, such as basic algebra. It took me fourteen hours of hard physical labor to give birth to one child; it took me three weeks of hard mental labor to give birth to basic algebra. During both events, I was definitely not an agreeable person.

The internal obstacles that I have encountered seem so great at times that my very soul screams to give up my dream. If it were not for the burning hunger for knowledge, I probably would have conceded and quit. I compare this strong desire to learn to that of a person who is blind in sight, a person who sees a few sparks of light occasionally and is drawn to them. I have lived my life in a darkness of mind, but I will not continue to do so. Before I began my courses in college, my reading comprehension skills were above normal, yet I scored lower grades than most due to my vocabulary. In previous years, I had taught myself to pay close attention to the sentence as a whole to understand the written meaning of a word. When the same word was set aside, I could not comprehend the definition. Today, I have discovered the use and have applied the tools of dictionaries, thesauruses and encyclopedias to enrich the meanings and concepts of the singular words and to bring more life into the sentences of the past. I sit down at night to read them, explore their worlds and create a broader horizon for my mind.

There are times when, in my eagerness and hunger for knowledge, that I push beyond my limited capabilities. My head feels as if my brain is swelling, and I become tired and angry with myself at the slow pace I seem to be progressing in. That is when I fight against my lack of understanding even harder with more study until exhaustion sets in and I am unable to fight anymore. On many late nights, I have heard a voice within me saying, "Why don't you just give up? Why put yourself through this torture?" But then I visualize a baby chick trying to burst out of its egg. I can almost hear the sound it makes while chipping away at the confining encasement. I rest for a while, find a temporary outlet to take my mind off my tiring fight, and begin anew hours later. I have a brain capable of learning, but was denied the opportunity as a youth. Stupid I am not! I am merely unlearned.

I am forty-five years old. Taking into consideration as to how much time I will need to get my degree in secondary education, I will be in or near my early fifties when I venture forward into the employment market. The length of time that I can hope to perform in my chosen field will be less than my fellow graduates. Although our nation has established a law protecting everyone from age discrimination, it is often neglected and ignored by employers. Still, I do possess one qualification over my younger colleagues: I fully understand what it is to live as a high school drop-out. To have to accept employment that brings only a meager existence, both financially and socially, is demeaning. This hateful, dreadful fate is one I long to fight against. I want to cheat this darkness of mind by reaching as many teenagers as I can before they, too, learn the depth of the pit of ignorance.

Leo Solvick

My name is Leo Solvick. I am a thirty-two-year-old truck driver, married, and I have six children. With the encouragement of my wife and my boss, I signed up for classes at Muskegon Community College in the fall of 1992. I would like to convey to you some of my personal challenges and obstacles which I encountered before and after I did this.

Prior to signing up for courses at M.C.C., my greatest challenge was convincing myself that I could do it. I had several excuses as to why I couldn't do it. For instance, I would think to myself about how I wasn't a very good student back in high school. My grades in high school left a lot to be desired—C's or D's were about the extent of it, other than maybe art or shop class. Also, when I was in high school, I didn't want to be there; I didn't like going to school. I wanted to get school over with so I could go to work full-time and get my life rolling. Another excuse was that I don't like to read or write. When I was in high school, I would do just enough reading to get me through the classes without failing. When I would write an assignment, I always did the minimum, never more and never less, just enough to pass the classes.

Another challenge I encountered was deciding what I wanted to go into. I have been driving trucks since I was sixteen years old, and I have always enjoyed it. But I started getting tired of the long hours and the loneliness of the job. Also, I would look back on the past years and think about how I had missed watching my children grow up because I was always working. That started me thinking about what else I could do. What would I want to do? I decided I would like to go into welding and become a maintenance man at the shop where I work. However, since the maintenance shop had a full crew, it could be years before I would be able to get into maintenance. My second choice was business management, but when we had a meeting at work and they announced that they were reducing the management staff by five persons, I scratched that idea!

I really like the company I work for because the benefits are good as well as the working conditions, so I really wanted to learn something I could go into and still work for the same people. One day I was talking to my boss, and I asked him, "Bill, what can I learn to do that I can stay employed here, but not have to wait twenty years to get into a new department?"

He said, "How about data processing? Maintenance needs someone to work on the computers entering data on the down time of the machines." That was when I decided to go into data processing.

I found obstacles inside myself that I had to overcome. For example, I feared that I was too old to be going to college. After all, I am thirty-two years old, and I've been out of high school for fourteen years. Most of the students at M.C.C. are teenagers, and here I am in my thirties. After going to college for a while, I started to see more and more adult students my age and older. Since the fact that I was older didn't seem to bother the younger students at all, that fear has since diminished. I also worried that I wouldn't be able to keep up with the work and get good grades. Because of my poor grades in high school, I figured that in college nothing would be different, even if I tried harder than I had in high school. For the past fourteen years, the most I would read was street signs or how much a cheeseburger was. I wasn't interested in books or newspapers; I was too busy driving trucks. Therefore, the thought of a five-hundred-page textbook was pretty scary for me. Being afraid of failing created yet another obstacle that I had to overcome. For years I have been lecturing my children about getting good grades in school. What would they think if I were to fail a class or get D's and E's? Furthermore, if I were to fail a class or classes, my self-esteem would be damaged for life. I would have to cover my face to be around any of my family or friends.

But, with the constant praising of my work from my writing instructor, Mrs. Kelly, and my reading instructor, Mrs. Beukema, and my good test grades, the fear of not being able to keep up with the work or get good grades has subsided. However, at the end of my first semester, I was afraid of what was going to happen to my wallet. When I started college, my employer was paying 100 percent of my tuition and books. Three days before my tuition was due, I was informed that my employer would pay only 75 percent of my tuition, and I had to pay the other 25 percent. Having been laid off the week before, I didn't have any money because I hadn't received any unemployment check; yet I work second shift and don't get out of work until 1:00 P.M., so that left only two days for me to come up with the rest of my tuition. First I tried to borrow the money, but it was too close to Christmas for anyone to help me. Finally, I ended up selling my C.B. radio to cover the tuition for my next semester.

I also found obstacles outside myself that I needed to deal with. For instance, I work full-time, putting in forty hours a week or more (usually anywhere from 48 to 72 hours a week). On top of that, I live sixty miles away from work. In other words, I end up having to drive one and a half hours one way to work. I usually give myself an extra hour or so in case I break down or something. Therefore I'm usually away from home twelve hours a day, and it ends up even longer if I work more than eight hours a day. With that being the situation, I don't have much time with my family as it is, and going to college makes it even less. For example, on Sunday I was sitting at the dining room table doing my homework when my wife sat down next to me and wanted to talk to me. She said that I was spending too much time on my writing assignments and that she would appreciate having some of my attention for an hour or two. Likewise, the children started complaining that I wasn't there for them as I was before I started going to college. My daughters were in the Thanksgiving Day parade, and they wanted me to go and watch them, but I had six chapters to finish for one of my English classes. My son wanted me to go hunting with him, but I had to turn him down because I had two essays to have done for class the next day. Also my social life had just about ceased to exist. I don't get much any more other than going to work or classes at the college.

Occasionally, I would take my wife visiting, but not for very long. For instance, one Sunday she wanted to go visit her uncle, who lives a little over an hour from our house. We got there and had visited about a half an hour, and I told her we would have to get going because I had two chapters of work to get done. Another time I took her to Wal-Mart shopping, and we weren't there fifteen minutes before I had to tell her to hurry so I could get home and get my homework done. One good thing came of that shopping trip: it was the least costly ever!

Starting college for me meant persuading myself that I could do it, overcoming the fears inside myself, and dealing with the obstacles outside myself. To get to where I want to go, I must keep dealing with the hurdles and jump right into the classes with a positive attitude. That way I can reach the degree I want and get started in the career that I have chosen.

Donna Garriott

In fall 1991 my husband John burned both his eyes at work. He was welding, and sparks flew into his eyes. He had to wear patches over both eyes for three days. At that point I began to wonder what would happen to us if my husband could never see again. I didn't want to live off public aid and the government as I do now. I had only an eleventh grade education. Getting a job to provide for my family would be impossible. A friend of mine told me the government would pay for me to go back to school and get a college education. When I heard this, I prayed and asked my gracious God if I could go back to school. I went to Middle Tennessee State University and filled out the registration forms and financial aid papers. I then went to Nashville to get my GED. I was so nervous because I knew my future depended on passing the test. Before I passed the GED test, I was accepted into Middle Tennessee State University. I knew then my God had said yes. It wasn't as easy as I thought it would be to go back. I had to work around three major obstacles, food stamps, rent, and time spent at home.

My family has lived off food stamps for five years. It hasn't been easy, but we get by month to month. When I decided to go back to school, public aid cut my food stamps by seventy-five dollars. I worked around this by eating a lot more hot dogs and dried beans than before they cut my food stamps. I received one thousand eighty-five dollars for school. Eight hundred dollars went for tuition, two hundred dollars for books, and three hundred dollars for child care for my four-year-old daughter. I was left owing one hundred fifteen dollars, and public aid cut my stamps. I tried to get help with child care cost, but because I was married and my husband worked, I wasn't eligible to get any help. Public Aid didn't care how much my husband made; they were just concerned that he was making something, so we couldn't get help. Every semester I go to school, I have to report all help I get financially, and they cut my food stamps every time. I figure by the time I'm a sophomore, I will not get any help from Public Aid. Every semester I have to take a day off from school just to go and turn in papers and get reevaluated.

We live in government housing, so anytime there is a change in our finances, we have to report it. When I went back to school, I had to report it to my landlady. She raised my rent by nine dollars a month and said she wasn't finished raising it yet. I took out a Stafford loan to help with bill collectors that were suing me for payment. This semester I'm afraid my landlady will raise my rent more because of the Stafford loan. Then I won't be able to pay bills with the money; I will have to pay rent and buy more food. We have learned to work around this by buying cheaper products, such as cheaper laundry soap, dish soap, bar soap, and shampoo. I don't get to spend as much on my children as I would like to, but we're trying to survive the best way we know how. My children are in desperate need of clothes and shoes without holes in them. They will have them in the fall of 1993 when my now five-year-old daughter goes to school. Then I won't have to pay for child care and can use that money for clothes and shoes.

Time spent with my family is valuable time. I have a five-year-old daughter and a twelve-year-old son. They get bored very easily, so I usually play games with them: Yahtzee, cards, and aggravation. We take walks and go to church three times a week. I have a three-bedroom house and six people in my household. I am an immaculate housekeeper. Since I've gone back to school, I haven't had much time to spend with my children, and my home has become very dusty and messy. Everyone in my home has helped to work around these problems. My children clean their rooms; my brother-in-law cleans the living room; my husband cooks and does dishes twice a week; my mother has lunch done every day and washes, dries, and folds the laundry. The time spent with my children has suffered the most. I really miss playing games with them and going for walks. I study so much in college I don't have much time for them anymore, but they understand, and on Saturday and Sunday we spend the whole day together.

I thought I was too old to go back to school. I was twenty-eight years old, but I was determined to make a change in my life. I have been under a lot of stress since I have gone back to school because I want to learn all I can and become a good nurse. I want to be able to provide a good home and environment for my family. It hasn't been easy going back to college, but I am determined to get my BSN. I have told my husband if we have to live in a tent, wear rags for clothes, have no shoes, and eat grass for food, I'm going to stay in school. Since I have been in school and loved going to my classes, my children have been encouraged to get involved in school projects and do the best they can in their school. I got very frustrated with the government programs that help provide for my family because I thought they would rather have me trying to get off the programs than living off of them the rest of my life. The only hope I have of a good future depends on my graduating from Middle Tennessee State University.

Jama Bile

Around the world, a lot of students face many different problems, which most of the time persuade them not to continue their educations. I myself was one of those students who faced obstacles. My reasons were physical problems, mental problems, and financial problems.

I was lucky that I didn't have many external problems. When I came to the United States from Somalia, I was sixteen years old; I lived with my brother in Virginia. We got along well at the beginning, but after a while we found that we had very different personalities. We started arguing with each other constantly, which almost ended our relationship. There were many times when I slept with an empty stomach because there was no food in the house and my brother never gave me any money. It was at that point that I decided to work on or solve all the problems that were keeping me and my brother apart. I did it, not because I wanted to or was interested in solving the problem, but so I could get my three meals a day.

In addition to my physical problems, I also had some mental problems. My biggest one was the civil war going on in my country, Somalia. It was hard for me to concentrate on my studies because I was always hearing some bad news from my country and my family. When the civil war started, my family left Mogadishu, and we didn't hear from them for about three months. For those three months, I hardly slept or ate. There was often bad news from my relatives. One time my brother was informed that eleven of our close relatives (first cousins, nephews, nieces, uncles and aunts) had died trying to cross the sea between Somalia and Kenya. Another time two of my cousins and my uncle got killed trying to protect themselves. However, my brother delayed telling me because he knew it would hurt me and would also interfere with the exams that I had to take that week.

Another problem that almost made me not go to college was the language. I came to the United States without speaking any English at all. I couldn't communicate with the teacher or even the students. There were many times when I wanted to purchase something, but I wasn't able to express myself in English. During that time, I was bored, lonely, and sometimes depressed. There was one time when my friend and I went running, and while we were running about three miles, very strong rain started and we couldn't find the house. We tried to talk to some people to ask directions, but they didn't understand what we were saying. Even though it took us nearly five hours, we finally found the house after the rain stopped. It was very hard to learn the language, and many times quitting school came to my mind. Learning the language wasn't easy. It took me about three years to understand English very well. The best way I learned the language was by hanging out with American kids and totally avoiding talking to the people from my country.

In addition to those physical and mental problems, I also had financial problems. I came from a poor family, and I was very sure that my parents wouldn't be able to pay for my college tuition. My parents couldn't even support themselves. My brother, who is a professional runner, did everything he could for me. He sent me to a private school and paid for my tuition, but he couldn't afford to pay for my college tuition because he was helping all of my family and relatives in Somalia, who had even more serious problems caused by the war.

I figured out that the only way I could go to college was to get a scholarship. I began working hard on my running. I used to run a little when I was in my country, but I wasn't very serious about it. So I started running hard, and I became one of the top runners in this nation during my junior year in high school. My senior year was a disaster. I ran my worst, which caused all the schools that were interested in me to stop writing and calling. I finally talked to George Young, the cross country Coach at Central Arizona College, and he gave me a scholarship. If it weren't for my running and for Coach Young, I wouldn't be here today. But today I'm the number one man on the team for cross country. I won many races, such as the regionals, and I finished fifth at the nationals.

While I was going through all these problems, I also decided on some goals to achieve for the future. The first goal is to get an education, something most of my family hasn't had the opportunity to get. My second goal is to major in something that I can take back to my country and help those needy people. I am planning to become a teacher or a doctor. I am doing this partly for myself and partly to help my country and my people. My third goal is to become an Olympic champion one day in the 1500 meters.

I faced a variety of problems that almost made me not go to college, such as physical problems, mental problems, and financial problems. But because of faith and my will to get to school and to get an education, I survived all of those oppositions. I have many goals for myself, and hopefully I will succeed.

Anita Werry

Nothing comes easily. If it did, I suspect life would be boring and without challenge. In school, I remember reading and very much enjoying the writings of Ralph Waldo Emerson. Touching many points of interest and encouragement, Emerson has certainly stimulated and motivated me in all I have dreamed of accomplishing. At one time I believe I might have accepted the hand dealt to me in this life. Thank God for that spark of inspiration that continued to burn inside of me until at last I said, "It is time I take charge of my own life." Emerson writes in his essay "Self-Reliance":

> There is a time in every man's education when he arrives at the conviction that envy is ignorance; that imitation is suicide; that he must take himself for better, for worse, as his portion; that though the wide universe is full of good, no kernel of nourishing corn can come to him but through his toil bestowed on that plot of ground which is given to him to till. The power which resides in him is new in nature, and none but he knows what that is which he can do, nor does he know until he has tried.

When growing up, I can remember so vividly the envy I felt when others would talk about their mothers and fathers. A father-daughter relationship was one I never experienced. It was not until I was fifteen years old that I was introduced to my father; consequently, any kind of relationship never developed. The connection between myself and my mother was unusual. Discipline was scarce and worse, not a true foundation was constructed that would present and promote a secure future. I feel that success, as well as character, are necessary ingredients in a role model that need to exist, but that never did in my case. This role model not only teaches us how to meet our difficulties face to face, but also teaches us how to be in charge of our own lives. Furthermore, an appropriate role model is imperative to the successful and complete molding of a young person's existence. I sometimes wonder how different my life would be today if I had had this role model.

In addition to having a role model, empowerment must be a part of this learning process we call experience and should be together at one's side with consistency and discipline. Certainly, being reared in a single-parent home did not need to be, but nevertheless was, a struggle to survive poor economic conditions. For me it was a battle with intense insecurities and a tremendous attempt for the one and only desire that is important to us all—to be accepted. A memory I recall the most when I remember my childhood experiences is never really feeling accepted.

If education were of interest to me, at all events, school was not encouraged. Independence in company with self-reliance was not promoted, and therefore interests that were not of the best choice took control in my early adult years. Being a high school dropout at the age of seventeen, I soon found myself a mother at the age of eighteen. Believing that "new" was better than "hand me downs," I was eager to start earning the almighty dollar. I truly believed that if I were employed with dedication, responsibilities in position would soon follow. This was my picture of financial success. Having mixed feelings about my situation and so undecided as to the road I should follow, again I found that surviving poor economic conditions would play a major role in every step I took. Now I not only had myself to consider, but the life and molding of another human being. Within three months, I was alone to handle the choice for myself. Emerson writes, "... and truly it demands something godlike in him who cast off the motives of humanity and has ventured to trust himself for a task master." Individuality is recognized in this statement and portrays Emerson's self-reliance. Emerson continues to encourage this by saying, "High be his heart, faithful his will, clear his sight, that he may in good earnest be doctrine, society, law to himself that a single purpose may be to him as strong as iron necessity is to others."

I suppose there was a part of me that felt imprisoned, trapped, and frightened. Although these feelings did exist, my strong obsession to succeed dominated my life. I needed to break away from the tradition that smothered any hope of escape. I attempted to return to school by enrolling in an evening class so that, at the very least, I could earn my high school diploma. The situation was difficult with a house to keep, children to take care of, and a job to work part-time; all of these responsibilities were very demanding on my time. Most importantly, I was extremely fortunate to have in my life an exceedingly remarkable and notably supportive spouse.

The situation brought true meaning to the word independence. There was too much to do, and I needed more than a twenty-four hour day to complete all that was required of me. Any sight of deliverance seemed blurred. This was not what I expected. As a result of my not-so-wise choices in early adult life, I was unable to finish school at this time. Unequivocally, unmistakably, and without a doubt, I was devastated at the admittance of defeat. Working and mothering full time was overtime.

I went on for ten years, almost convinced that this was the way it was, the way it is, and the way it was always going to be. I chose the path to follow, and it was learned early on: accept and live the road you have chosen. Never did I understand what it was to be in charge of my own life. Why did I have to accept this? Why was I conditioned to believe there were no other alternatives? What was my worth? Thanking God, realizing that I did not have to accept this chosen road and there was a better and definite path for me in whatever I might choose, I was compelled to succeed. Not an obstacle would I allow in my path that somehow I would not find my way around, even if it meant to tackle the barricade head on. My high school diploma was earned in less than one month. The completion of this task only made me hungry for another challenge. If I were able to accomplish this, what else was I capable of?

Remembering when I was small, the desire to doctor in some capacity was always a moving appetite in my heart. For me, like a piece of chocolate satisfying that incredible desire for candy, helping others was a satisfying blanket of warmth wrapped around my heart. Because of not believing in myself and the lack of support and encouragement, the only nurturing I found was from my immediate family. Now it was time for me to allow myself to pursue the longing I had to help others. What interested, fascinated and satisfied me the most? Would my choices be rewarding to not only myself but to others? How could I make a difference in society? How could I empower another human being and still be that support he or she might need?

Is it not quaint that I myself required some special educational assistance in my early school years? Today I am employed by a special education school for mentally handicapped children. The school attends to the needs of children with numerous and various disabilities. The experience with my involvement has only been positive. Among other challenges, I am involved in building self-esteem and have been an asset not only to the children I serve, but I am also a therapist in treating my own insecurities. The environment here only clears my vision when

I see a student conquer a goal he or she has worked so vigorously to achieve. Nothing worth achieving is without toil.

Recently I have made inquiries about different schools and the opportunities in the advancement of education. After several placement tests, I found myself involved in the Academic Foundations program at Shepherd College in Shepherdstown, West Virginia. My first class in my return to school was a developmental course in critical composition (a basic writing class). If I did not learn anything else, I learned confidence. The learning experience, in my estimation, was incredible. A spark inside of me grew into a raging fire so intense with the burning desire to learn that not a well could drown it out. After this developmental course, I was headed for a mathematics class. Honestly, If I could overcome this arduous task, I was convinced I was material for anything I attempted to achieve. I was triumphant! I could surmount or whip at hand any obstacle that moved my way. Furthermore, I now cannot conceive there was a time that education did not intrigue me. After all, education is an impeccable gift that should be seized by all who are capable.

I still struggle with my insecurities, but I am learning to appreciate life and all that it has to offer. I am able to survive in the economic condition that has been laid before me now, and I accept who I am more readily, believing that each of us has a gift to share with another. The choice is ours as to whether or not we choose to share this wonderful gift. Sometimes weathering the storm becomes wearisome, and sometimes discouragement is difficult for us to overcome. It is so marvelous a feeling when that dull light brightens and the storm is calming, defeat diminishes, and victory stands strong!

Sandy Wagner

I sit in my dining room looking at the mess strewn around the room. I call this my office. The table is covered with an assortment of books, pens, and paper. Hanging on the back of a chair is my black leather book bag. I am finally a college student. The kids are gone, my husband works away from home all week, and the dogs are asleep. My house is finally quiet. I can study and read all day if I want to. There is no one yelling "What's for dinner?" or "Did you see my red sweater?" I can leave my papers lying on the table without the fear of peanut butter stains or someone spilling a Pepsi on them. I even have my own spending money. No more penny-pinching to buy a prom gown or a class ring. I can practice my speeches aloud without hearing snickers or giggling behind my back. If I want to wear my jeans with the worn knees or my angora sweater, I know it is in my closet, just where I left it. Nobody borrowed it without permission.

For the first time in twenty-eight years, I have no one to take care of but myself. The only report card I agonize over is my own. For years my days were filled with laundry, cleaning, cooking and helping seven children achieve their dreams. For years I got up at the crack of dawn, making sure the younger kids got on the bus and that the older ones got their cars started, quietly standing by and holding my breath, hoping I wouldn't have to drive anyone to school.

It seems like I spent half of those twenty-eight years sitting in the principal's office listening to him tell me that my two boys were destined to become mass killers. It didn't matter if their offense was as small as waving to a teacher with their middle finger; the principal always acted like they had just robbed a Seven-Eleven. As the years went by, one by one they graduated and left home, and I would rejoice inside. I let them think my life couldn't go on without them, but inside I was singing "Zippity Doo Da."

When I got down to the final child, my boy Jamie, I decided it was my turn at life. When Jamie was a senior, I decided I would attempt my life-long dream. I would become a nurse. My mind kept saying, "You're an old woman." The next day that same mind would say, "You're not that old; you're only forty-five." I knew the journey would not be an easy one since I had not graduated from high school. I married at seventeen and started my family at the age of nineteen. I didn't know how to do anything but be a mother. My composition skills had not been challenged by anything harder than making up an excuse for the boys, describing one of the many diseases they swore they had when they missed a day of school. My imagination hadn't been used for anything except all the things I imagined my boys doing in the back seats of their cars or the things I imagined other boys trying to talk my girls into in the back seat of a car.

I had very little self-esteem, and I didn't feel very smart. I knew I had to take my GED test in order to get into college. With much anxiety I began classes to prepare me for the test. Finally the day came; my mind was in an uproar thinking, "What if I fail? I'll be so embarrassed if I fail." After all the lectures I gave the kids on the importance of grades, how could I explain to them if I failed? Maybe it wasn't as easy as I told them it was. My palms were sweaty as I sat down at my desk, my knees were shaking, and I had to go to the bathroom. The instructor passed out pencils and the test booklets. He looked at the clock and told us to begin. He was a tall, lanky man who looked like Ichabod Crane. His silly appearance and relaxed attitude put me at ease. I figured if someone like Ichabod could pass this test, I surely had a chance. I looked at the first question. I actually knew the answer! With excitement in my heart, my shaky hand marked the correct answer! I looked at questions two, three and four. I knew those answers also. On the entire test there were only a handful of questions that I couldn't answer correctly. I handed in the test and waited for it to be corrected. In the next ten minutes, I paced like a caged lion and went to the bathroom three times. Finally he told me the test results. I had passed with flying colors. The instructor told me that only a few people each year score as high as I did.

That was all the encouragement I needed. I went home and got out all of the literature I had on colleges. I had made up my mind: I was going. I filled out the registration form and sent in my fee. In a few weeks the mailman brought the letter I was waiting for. I had been accepted, and I would start classes in August. I was taking the first step of my journey.

The summer before I started college, I got more nervous as the weeks went on. I was having some health problems which required surgery. In the three months of summer, I had three major operations. Many times I became discouraged, and I was physically exhausted from the surgery. I couldn't imagine myself tramping all over the campus carrying a bag of books or sitting up half the night studying for a test. As I began to recuperate and my body grew stronger, my attitude once again became positive.

Finally, the summer ended and school began. I dressed in jeans and a sweatshirt and slung my book bag over my shoulder and set out for my first class. The butterflies in my stomach felt like elephants marching around inside of me. I found my first class and sat down. I looked around and thought, "My God, they are just babies. I must look like a wrinkled, pathetic, old antique to them." It didn't take long for me to realize they didn't care about my age. I was just one of them, a student. As the days went on and the professors gave the assignments, I raced home and began my homework. My mind came up with ideas that amazed even me. My classmates seemed genuinely interested in the essays, and the professors acted as if I had something worthwhile to contribute. I was having the time of my life.

The semester is coming to a close. I look upon it with sadness. I will miss my teachers and the friendships I have made. I am looking forward to next semester, but I also get nervous thinking about my new classes. Each semester the classes will get a little harder and more challenging. I hope I am up to all those new challenges. I love to learn, but I still have a little fear of failing. If the professors are as helpful and encouraging as they were last semester, it will help a lot. At my age a little encouragement can make the difference between quitting or marching forward.

I guess the difference between someone my age and the younger students is that I know that you usually only get one chance at something. It is a very serious thing to me. It is very expensive to go to college, too expensive to waste. I try to do my very best in every class. Life is too short to waste even a minute of it, and the mind is too precious to waste even a thought. I am enjoying the responsibility of turning in my assignments and doing the many experiments. I am sure this will help me in my career as a nurse. I have always been very dependable, but I guess my life got easier with each child's leaving; I got a little lazy. It feels good to get up each morning with a purpose in mind. I look forward to each new day, and I look forward to the new friendships I will make each semester. I like the feeling of helping people and the feeling of accomplishing something. These traits will make me a good nurse. I already feel as though I have accomplished something, and I am only halfway there.

In two years I will be a registered nurse, a darn good one. I will have done something that didn't need to be done, something that I dreamed about doing and did. My journey will soon come to an end, and maybe I'll start a new one. Maybe I'll go to school two extra years and teach nursing. Who knows? Dreams can come true. They take hard work, but they can come true. Mine is getting more real each day.

Dave J. Hanson

The poem "Invictus" claims, "I am the master of my fate; I am the captain of my soul." We really are the masters of our own destiny. We shape our future by the way we take charge of our life. We hold the key to what lies ahead. Life is what we make it—a heaven or a hell on earth.

After finishing high school in 1984, I did not consider going to college. The new culture I got into, the new language I had to be adept in, and the new values I had to acquire did not hinder me from looking for a job. It didn't matter how low the pay was. All I aimed for was to earn money and enjoy the luxuries life could offer—nice clothes, shoes, and jewelry. I tried working in customer service, fast-food restaurants, department stores, and offices. I worked mornings, nights, and weekends to no avail. As years went by, I realized I was working myself to death with little success. I never got a raise or a promotion because I knew others proved to be more qualified than I was.

I woke up to a shocking reality one morning. I simply had to have a goal in life. I seemed to be going nowhere. That's when I thought of going back to school. With my meager savings and a student loan, I finally found myself attending a business school where I acquired basic skills in computer operations, math, English and typing. How proud I was to graduate at the top of my class.

Armed with a certificate and a young man's guts, I applied to countless advertisements in New York dailies. After weeks and months of job searching, I was finally interviewed for a data entry position. I met new people, had new friends, and savored the sights and lures of the Big Apple. I enjoyed my job and the income I had; I could afford to go out with friends for a few drinks and movies. Despite the happy times I had, I felt something was missing in my life. I looked around for factors that could mean success. I discovered all my bosses were successful in their chosen careers because they not only had college educations but MBA's and Ph.D's as well. Right then and there, I realized I needed a college degree. I must take college courses and get a better job. Feeling so academically inadequate and inspired by the role models of my superiors, I decided to enroll in a two-year course preparatory to nursing. With this decision I had, I began a rat race for education.

During early morning rush hours, I joined the hordes of humanity taking the PATH train to the World Trade Center. After a hard day to work, I had to take the train and the subway to reach my classes, which lasted up to 9:30 P.M. Our assignments were long and time-consuming, so I had to give up much of my lunch break and coffee breaks to do my homework. At times I ended up dozing on the train rather than fall asleep during class hours. With this kind of schedule, I realized I could not be a full-time student. Doing this would give me only a few credits per semester. It would take me years to get a degree. "Should I give up my job?" I asked myself.

The solution presented itself when recession touched New York City's real estate business. Our company suffered a big slump, and one by one the employees had to go. I was one of the last to leave with a heavy heart out of this skyscraper. The shock was too much, but I realized later this was a blessing in disguise.

At this critical point in my life, I yearned for drastic changes, for innovations that could make a better me. Luckily, I found a friend who gave me this advice: "When God closes a door, He opens a window." I came to my senses. I had to be jolted to realize that I should really work hard, take the challenge, try to live on my means, and make the most of what education could offer. My savings dwindled, and I had to apply for financial aid.

Now, several semesters later, I am at last physically and emotionally engrossed with my studies. Having a 12-credit course, I literally have no time to have a job, not even a part-time one. I got several calls and interviews. When my prospective employers saw my staggered schedule from 8:30 A.M. to 8:45 P.M., much as they wanted to, they agreed that it would be too much for me to work.

Now, as a freshman nursing student, I find myself in a constant struggle. I have to leave behind my social life, my love life, and my ball games in favor of A's and B's. I find all my courses are very challenging because I have to get an A+ in order to get into the nursing program. Therefore, I'm working so hard to get better grades because they are the good things that will push me to the career I want. All the subjects take most of my time—from morning till wee hours of the morning, even weekends, too. Anatomy and physiology keep me awake all night trying to remember anatomical and clinical terminologies, memorizing definitions, tracing flowcharts and diagrams, trying to find which bone and which tissues come from a particular disorder, etc. What is frustrating is trying to digest and remember as much as five to ten chapters in so short a time with the least help from my teacher. My English class has taught me how to do research paper and paragraph writing. With all the assignments, the readings, and the compositions we have to write, I really have to devote more time for it, too. My sociology class also involves reporting, researching, and reading in order to pass the course.

Life for me now is totally different. Here I am a full-time student, trying to make up for lost time, trying to make both ends meet with my financial aid, and spending sleepless nights over my load of books. I am in financial distress. I have matured a lot through the years. I have come to know the value of work and time. I know how valuable education is. I am not bothered by giving up my social life or love life for now. These things can come later when I am a full-fledged nurse. What inspires me is the desire to be a nurse, to help the sick, the needy, and aged. What my friend told me keeps on coming back every time I feel like giving up. I hope God would open a window for me now that a door has closed. I need a form of scholarship to keep me going next semester. Will you open the door for me?

Fred Balmer

For the first time in twenty-eight years, I feel like I am taking charge of my life. On July 9, 1992, I began my first college course. Many may say this is not a major accomplishment, but to someone with learning disabilities, this step was the hardest step to take. Learning disabilities have held me back for years, and they have not and will not go away. I am struggling to learn in spite of these setbacks.

One of the earliest challenges I remember about school is the second grade. Spelling tests had become a nightmare! No one had ever sat down and explained to me what a spelling test was. I did not study my words and would cry during tests because I did not know what to do. I feel this was the beginning of when my learning disabilities surfaced. I was retained in second grade and was placed into a resource class in the third grade for a small part of each day.

The next challenge I had to face was overcoming part of my home life. I was quite a bit younger than my brothers and sisters, and they set a poor example for me to follow. When my problems were first beginning to surface, my brothers and sisters were just dropping out of school. I was developing an "I don't care" attitude. The importance of an education was never stressed in our home. My father worked days and my mother worked nights, so we did not have much family communication. My parents never helped me try to overcome my school problems early in life. I do not know if they just did not realize I had a learning problem or if they just did not have time to help me overcome my problems.

Another challenge of my home life was having to deal with the availability of drugs and alcohol. All my brothers and sisters were alcohol and drug users, so it was inevitable that I use them also. This was probably a major reason I did not do well in late elementary and junior high. During this time I was placed into resource classes for most of the day. The other resource children and I knew we were not as smart as everyone else. The resource room was located next to the special education room, and it was embarrassing to have to go there. Socially I kept up with all the other children my age, but mentally I could not keep up. This damaged my self-esteem at a very young age.

As I entered high school, the challenges I had to face had not disappeared. I entered athletics in the ninth grade, and I felt this helped me to stay in school and not quit. The reputation resource children had was that of being "stupid" or "dumb." I would wait until all my friends went to their classes; then I would hurry to resource. Dating was even worse! I was so scared someone I was dating would find out I was in resource classes or that I was "stupid." This stigma just about destroyed what little self-esteem I had left. I had absolutely no confidence in myself. Even things I could do well I would never give myself credit for doing. I wanted to have confidence, yet I could not seem to find it in anything. But somehow I found something inside me to enable me to finish school. Maybe it was because all my friends set a good example for me by staying in school. During these years I still used drugs and alcohol; I just did not let them take over my life. I did graduate from high school in May, 1983.

Once out of high school, I did odd jobs in the labor force and did fairly well for myself. Thoughts of a better education did cross my mind at times, but I knew I could never succeed at higher education. At age twenty-three, I became active in my church and shed all my unhealthy habits. My life was beginning to turn around, and I was controlling it. I served a two-year mission for my church, and this improved my reading skills and my self-esteem. Once home from my mission, I began a job at a construction company that paid really well. I got married about a year later. My wife was an education major and thought school was really important for everyone. We talked of my going to school and were working on my reading and math skills at home. Things seemed to be going really well for us, and my confidence was growing each day. Last New Year's Day I got laid off from my job, my wife had one more semester of college, and we were expecting a baby. Facing this challenge was almost more than I thought I could handle. We talked of my going to school, but there was not any way that I could do it at this time with all the financial responsibilities we had.

When my wife finished college and secured a teaching job, we knew this was the time for me to go to school. We filled out the paperwork, and I took the reading part of the TASP test (a test I had to pass to take college-level courses in Texas). I passed it! My grant papers got a little mixed up, but we finally got those straightened out. I registered for Summer II and took developmental math and psychology. The pressure and inadequacy I felt when I first entered that classroom cannot be described. Most of the students were about ten years younger than I was and used terms for things I had never heard of. Without the support of my wife, I could not have made it through those first few weeks. I studied really hard for my classes. My wife made notes from the lectures I recorded and read my textbook onto tape, yet I still struggled. I had the highest average in my math class, even though I had to drop my psychology class. I decided to become a registered nurse and continue the challenge. My classes in the fall were also tough, but I only had to drop one. I have learned many things since that first day.

I feel one of the hardest challenges I have to face is knowing that I have so much trouble making all the information go together. I also have to sit back and watch my wife work and make the money to support our family. With my learning disabilities, I am unable to work because I have to devote all my time to studying. My wife teaches all day and then comes home and tutors and helps me in the evenings.

I am presently working with the Texas Rehabilitation Commission. They will be helping me not only monetarily, but also with tutors to help improve my reading skills and my confidence in myself. I am getting all my textbooks on cassette tape through Recordings for the Blind. They help anyone with a disability. This will be a big help by helping my studying go more quickly and more efficiently. For the spring semester I am taking a study skills class, which will help me prepare for tests better since I have test anxiety.

Though I have met and faced many of the challenges to get into college, I still have many more challenges to face. I know that college probably will take me twice as long as most people. The learning disabilities I have will always be there, but I am learning more each day how to deal with them. I probably will always have test anxiety. I still have to pass the math and writing sections of the TASP test. I have an invalid mother, and I am responsible for most of her care, and my family still has to be provided for while I am in college.

As anyone can see, the challenges I have faced and have yet to face are numerous. I know with the continued support of my teachers at school, my wife, and the Texas Rehabilitation Commission, that I will eventually succeed and obtain a college degree. In the past year I have come from the back seat to the driver's seat and put myself in charge of my life. I make the decisions concerning me, and I am doing what I want to do for the first time in twenty-eight years.

Juan Angel

My name is Juan Angel. I am 30 years old, and I was born in Mexico.

As a child, I was alone for most of the time. My father was an alcoholic, and he abandoned my family and me when I was three years old. My mother had to struggle to survive by working from place to place in Mexico. Her good intentions to support me economically were not enough because of low salaries, so she eventually ended up working here in the United States.

I lived with some of my relatives in a little village in Mexico and worked from dawn to sunset and ate sometimes once a day. I felt totally condemned to die of starvation and hard work. My relatives spent the money that my mother sent me, claiming that I was just a child and didn't need it. As a defenseless child, I was innocent, ignorant, and lacked the courage to stand up against the abuse and the injustice. My Gramma, who lived in another little village, couldn't do anything about the oppression I suffered, and she probably didn't even know what was really happening in my life. My relatives covered everything up, and the complaints I made were ignored while my suffering continued to get worse. After five years of being mistreated, humiliated, and abused by my relatives, I decided to put an end to it, and I went to live with my Gramma.

When I moved into my Gramma's house, I started living a new lifestyle. By then, I was eight years old, and I felt for the first time proud of myself because I had made my first big decision in life.

My Gramma had some pigs, so I had to feed them. One day I was feeding them close to a water stream when I saw two boys passing by. They carried some books in their handbags. I saw them every day walking down a grassy road while I fed those pigs. My curiosity grew intensely, and one day I stopped them on their way back home. I asked them what they were doing, and they told me that they were attending school. I wanted to know if they knew how to read, and immediately they started reading and writing to show me. I simply couldn't believe it. When they left, I scratched my head and nodded for a moment, looking toward the sky. I said, "Going to school! That's exactly the next step I have to work on." After I finished feeding those pigs, I went home. While I was walking home, I thought about how I would convince my Gramma to allow me to to go school. I knew it was going to be hard to convince her because there were around twenty boys in the village, and they were not attending school either, except those two whom I admired.

When I talked to her about my decision on going to school, she got very upset, and she immediately thought about who would care for her pigs. I calmed her down by telling her that I would continue feeding them. She didn't accept my proposal at first, so I looked for the two boys and talked to them about my interest in going to school. They encouraged me to leave the house and forget about the pigs; they would help me to go. I thought it was not a bad idea, but I opposed it because my Gramma and I were living alone. In addition, the closest school was two miles away from the village. For those reasons I hesitated to make such a decision. I had spent two years growing pigs and hesitated about my next step.

Finally, I gave up and left my Gramma alone in the house. My friends helped me find a place to sleep in town where the school was, and they gave me some food every day. They took me to the school, and I explained my situation to the principal; to my surprise, his name was Juan, also. He told me that my age (ten years old) wouldn't match the rules of the school. "You're too old," he said. He questioned me for about five minutes, and then he told me to come back the next day. He met with all the teachers, and after some deliberation, they approved my enrollment as a new student. I was excited and happy about my achievement as a ten-year-old boy. On the other hand, I couldn't sleep very well at night because I remembered my Gramma very much. She was desperately looking for me, and she found me after a week. I cried while I explained to her why I had left home. She hugged me very hard, and then she went to talk to the principal about my desire to attend school. I never expected her to talk to the principal, but she did. I have never experienced so much happiness in my life as when I was ten years old.

I walked the two miles back and forth to school every day. In addition, I had to feed the pigs early in the morning before I went to school and after I came home from school. I also chopped wood for cooking. I did chores at home as a responsible man in charge of a household. My Gramma and I lived happily for six years while I was in primary school.

After I finished my first six years in school, I had to make another tough decision. I had to leave my Gramma completely alone because the secondary school I wished to attend was in another town about three hours away by bus. A few months before I took off, she began to suffer from an acute pain in her chest. I didn't want to leave her, but I did. I wanted to stay in school as much as I could. I used to visit her every weekend, but sometimes the lack of money made it impossible. When I started my second year in the school, I began to worry about my Gramma's health. Her chest pains were getting worse, and I received a letter in which she said that she missed me very much.

A week later a friend of mine was looking for me at the school. He told me that my Gramma was very sick. I immediately went to see her. She was lying down with a blanket on the floor. When she saw me, she hugged me very hard, and then she began to ask how my school was. I could hardly answer her because my tears ran down my cheeks as never before. She asked me not to cry, but I couldn't stop. She told me to continue in school, and I promised her I would. A few minutes later, she died in my arms, and I felt that everything was torn apart inside me. I thought that I could never overcome the painful experience of losing my Gramma forever.

My mother, who was here in the United States, got there in time for the funeral. She asked me to come with her, but I refused her offer. She came back to the United States, and I stayed in Mexico for another four years of school. She continued asking me to join her. Finally, I gave in and immigrated to the United States in 1988. I immediately attended an English class at night and worked days. At the end of the year I got here, my English teacher recommended me to a Hispanic program where I could get my GED diploma. When I enrolled in the program, everything was free, including a room in a dormitory. When I finished the program, I had my GED. I then returned to my mother's house. I was unemployed, and three months later, I started working on an irrigated farm, growing alfalfa. I worked three years, and I quit because I wanted to find a more flexible job which allowed me to go to college.

Now I'm working in a feed department on swing shift, and I'm attending college in the morning. This department where I'm working operates just in the wintertime, so I'm on the verge of being laid off.

I'm a part-time student at Blue Mountain Community College, and I would like to continue attending college. I will keep trying to find ways to stay in college.

I have been confronting many obstacles in my life since my childhood. I have challenged those obstacles, and I know by experience how to overcome them. It has not been easy, but I always believe in success through education. Even though I know the struggle is not over yet, I will keep an optimistic smile toward the future.

Andrew Drahos

College is a big step in the life of anybody. For most, it is a time to discover who we are and what we want from our lives. For a few it is an opportunity to expand on what has already been accomplished. For whatever reason people go to college, there are usually obstacles for everyone to overcome. I am no exception to this. There have been several different obstacles both inside and outside of myself that had to be overcome before getting a college education.

I am a twenty-nine-year-old junior attending Utica College of Syracuse University. My major is construction management, and my goal is to work for a large construction or architectural firm in or near New York City. Eventually, I want to have my own construction company concentrating on single-family homes. Prior to Utica College I received an associate's degree from Ulster County Community College in drafting and design. In addition, I served three years in the United States Marine Corps, where I was a field radio operator. I also have two and a half years experience in land surveying and two years experience as a carpenter. I want to get a college education to expand on my knowledge and experience in the surveying and construction fields. This has not been an easy road.

Having a positive attitude toward learning did not exist for me in high school. Getting an education was not always a priority in my life. All through high school I did not think an education was important. What was important was hanging out and partying. I did not make a strong effort in any of the classes. Doing the minimum amount of work necessary to make it through was good enough. There was not anything anybody could say or do to change my mind. No matter how many attempts were made, I would not change. My attitude was, "I am going into the Marine Corps, so I do not need high school." Developing the attitude needed for college seemed impossible for me to achieve.

It was not until after spending time in the Marine Corps that I realized it should be a priority of mine to get a college education. In the

Marine Corps the people in charge tell you when and how to do everything, especially in basic training; they told you when and how to eat, sleep, go to the bathroom, walk, exercise, and even learn. Being constantly supervised and told what to do was an everyday thing. That was their way of giving people discipline. It did not take long at all for me to realize what I had to do and when to do it. The fact that I was being paid for learning a skill made me want to learn even more about my job. It became clear to me that civilian life was the same way. I finally understood the importance of getting an education. It was the help and discipline of the Marine Corps that gave me the right attitude for getting an education.

The fear of leaving work to go to college had to be overcome. It was possible to get carpentry and land surveying jobs with just a high school education and military experience. They were not the best paying jobs, but it was comfortable knowing that I at least had a job. Now that I had the attitude and strong desire for getting an education, going to night classes part-time was not good enough. I knew if I wanted to go to college, it had to be full-time. For four years, the time for deciding to go to college came and went. Going to college was going to take either forcing myself or being forced by someone else. Fortunately or unfortunately, tragedy struck which forced me to make a major decision. An accident on the job put me out of work for three weeks. I soon healed and was able to go back to work, but the company I worked for decided I was not needed. I had to decide which was more beneficial, finding another job or going to school. The fact that our nation was in the middle of a recession, and any jobs I had experience for were not available, made deciding to go to college easier. Finally, after four years of waiting, the opportunity for me to go to college was here, and I was taking it. It took an accident at work and being forced to make a decision to overcome the fear of leaving work to get an education.

The work load and level of learning needed for college had me feeling very intimidated. I did not know if I was able to handle college. The learning atmosphere at college is very different than that of high school. Knowing that I was not a very good high school student had me extremely scared. I was afraid of not being able to do the work; or if I was able to do it, keeping up with the work was going to be impossible. During high school, the attitude and the effort were not there. Now that the attitude was there, I had to use that and put out a lot of effort. As time went on, I discovered that a good attitude and a strong effort were all that I needed to be in college. Not only was I able to do and keep up with the work, I was also getting good grades. The good grades made me feel good about myself and gave me more confidence and desire to continue. It did not take very long to get comfortable and not feel intimidated about college.

Having personal expenses to take care of while going to college made it difficult to handle the work load of college. While working for a number of years after high school, several personal expenses built up. Now that I was going to college, a part-time job at night was necessary to have the finances available to pay those expenses, not to mention the finances needed for college. Luckily, I had a part-time job at night and on weekends before my accident which I was able to keep. Having the job was good, but it took away from time needed to do class work. There was no time for anything else, but anything else was not necessary. The only important thing was going to college and having the necessary finances. While it was not easy, having a part-time job in the evening gave me the time necessary to keep up with the work load of college.

Determining how much education to get was the next obstacle to overcome. Before I started going to college, and even after I was going for the first year, it seemed like an associate's degree in drafting and design would be enough. As I got closer to finishing the first year of college, I started thinking that I would not be satisfied with just a two-year degree. Even while I was working, I knew at some point in my life, starting my own construction business was what I wanted most. A two-year drafting degree would not be enough education necessary to start my own construction company. Going for more of an education to get at least a bachelor's degree seemed inevitable. While in my third semester, I started looking for a college to go to for a bachelor's degree in construction management. For what I wanted to do with my life, a two-year degree was not enough. More education was definitely needed.

Deciding to transfer to a four-year college made it difficult to focus on finishing the last semester for an associate's degree. Finding a college to apply to that had a construction management degree program was not very hard. I found that Utica College of Syracuse University had what I wanted. Filling out the application and writing an essay was time-consuming and a little difficult, but for the most part, it was no major problem. During the entire time of looking for and applying to Utica College, it was extremely difficult to concentrate on the classes I was still taking. I had been worried about getting accepted to U.C. I did not think I would be denied because I had a GPA of 3.25 at the time. At the same time, I was looking forward to going to Utica College. It would help me achieve my goal of starting my own business. I was just so excited because it seemed as though my life finally had more of a definite direction. This made it very difficult to stay focused on finishing the work necessary to get the associate's degree.

Making the decision of moving away from the comforts of home and my fiancée took a lot of consideration. Having to get used to a new place and new people makes moving away from home difficult. It does not take very long to get used to a new place. What would take a long time to get used to is being away from my main source of moral support, my fiancée, Barrie. All during the first two years of getting my associate's degree, Barrie was there for me every day if I had a bad day in a class or if I felt that I had done poorly on a test. She constantly reminded me that getting a degree was important and I should not quit. When I received good grades, she was there to tell me that I was doing well and she was proud of me. I had enough confidence in myself, but when someone whom you care about very much says you are doing well, and they are proud of you, it makes you try even harder. Going away to college and not being so close to the support was going to be difficult for me. Again, Barrie made me see that going to college was the most important thing for me and, in the long run, for both of us. Being apart was not going to be so bad. Occasional phone calls and visits from each other would help. The concern and support would always be there one way or another. Going away to college is the only way for me to get the degree I need for what I want to do. We have to make the best of it. While the phone calls and visits are not the same as being there all of the time, they do help very much and make being away bearable.

Having to live with other students that are eight to ten years younger than I was a difficult adjustment to make. The first time away from home for anybody is difficult. For as difficult as it is, most people do not take long adjusting to it. Typically, the first-time college student is eighteen years old. For most of them, being away from home and from Mom and Dad means party time, partying that goes on every night, all night. I had heard stories about college dorm life, but I did not think it would be so bad because I saw similar partying in the military. I did not remember that it had been seven years since I did any of that partying and while I was away from it, I changed. While I was not above that sort of behavior, I sure was beyond it. Realizing that I was only one person, there was no way I could stop the partying from going on. It became apparent to me, I would be the one to make the adjustments. Going to the library and other quiet places to study became necessary for me to adjust to the younger crowd.

Discovering a learning disability has added even more fear that I am not able to handle the work load of college. The first week into this past semester, I had difficulty with reading material that was given during a class. I approached the professor about the problem I was having immediately after the class. With the help of the academic support office on campus, it was discovered that I was reading on a ninth grade level. It was then necessary for me to make a class schedule change from one English class to a remedial English class. Up to that point in college, all of the work was technical. The only reading I had to do was looking for specific information. Now I have to read and understand complete chapters in less than a week. The academic support office has taught me the clustering method of note-taking while reading. I have not had to use it yet since most of the classes I had this semester were math or drawing classes. The English course did not require any reading except for the last assignment. Again, that reading was looking for specific information and was not very difficult for me. I know that these types of classes will not last forever. It is in the upcoming semesters that I will have a lot of reading to do. This has gotten me back to worrying about not being able to handle the work load of college. Discovering a learning disability has not been an obstacle for me yet, but it is something that will have to be overcome in the semesters still ahead of me.

Being diagnosed with Crohn's disease has created a constant source of pain for me to deal with. The first week in October, 1991, in the middle of my third semester, I was taken to the hospital from work with severe abdominal pain. I spent the first three of six days in the hospital undergoing tests to find the cause of the pain. It was finally determined that I have what is called Crohn's disease. It is an inflammation which can and often does affect the entire digestive system. A cause and a cure for this disease are unknown. The only treatment is medication. Depending on the severity and types of pains experienced, different medications are prescribed. In most cases an operation to remove part of the inflamed area is inevitable. For me, the disease is present in my large intestine. I have to take two medications, asacol and prednisone, three times a day, and I will be taking this medication for the rest of my life. Not a day goes by where I do not feel some pain. Some days are worse than others.

Being diagnosed with Crohn's disease has also created a constant financial burden for me. As mentioned earlier, I am on medication for the rest of my life. This medication is very expensive, about $120 per month. Along with the medication, this disease also requires me to make doctor visits. I have made approximately thirteen doctor visits since being diagnosed. Doctor visits are also expensive, about fifty dollars each visit. I do not have any medical insurance. In addition, because it is a pre-existing condition, getting medical insurance is impossible. Without the aid of insurance, I have to pay for the medication and doctor visits on my own.

Getting a college education has become very important to me, so much so that I am not going to let anything stand in my way. I have found that with hard work and dedication, any obstacle, big or small, can be overcome. I have had some help and support from a few people close to me. A scholarship from the Townsend Press Scholarship Program would be very helpful. In the end, it is up to me to get the education I want. Believe me, I want it.

LeQuita Foster

I have been asked to write an essay entitled "Taking Charge of My Life." I need to discuss the obstacles and challenges that have been and will be in my life concerning the goal that I have set for myself in the area of education. In order to write about these obstacles and challenges, I feel that I need to give a brief summary of my life. The reason I feel the need to do this is simple. I think that some of the obstacles that were put before me in my earlier years of life have made a lasting impact on how my life has turned out in my current years.

I am thirty-six years old. To my children, that is old. Well, let's see, three decades and six years. Boy, that does sound old, almost four decades. A person can come upon a number of obstacles and meet a great many challenges in four decades. In this essay I plan to take a look at each decade of my life up to and including the present.

My first decade in this world seemed to hold few obstacles and challenges, but the ones I did come up against would affect me for years to come. We were very poor when I was little, but until I started school, I don't believe I realized that. My first year in school was great. I had two brand-new dresses, and I was the teacher's pet. I did very well academically, and I had some very good friends. I felt like I was as "good" as any of the other children.

After my first year of school, my feelings about myself seemed to slowly change. The older I got, the more it seemed to matter where I was on the social ladder. This didn't seem to just matter to my classmates but to my teachers as well. It seemed to me that most teachers paid more attention to the popular kids.

I believe the summer I was eight years old I faced the most challenging obstacle of my entire life. I was molested that summer by two teenage boys. It took me two years before I could tell my parents, and it'll probably take me a lifetime to ever completely deal with it. I think this one obstacle has affected my life in some way every day since it happened. I'm also sure that it will continue to do so for many years to come.

My second decade held more challenges and obstacles than the first decade, but probably none so traumatic. I didn't do as well academically in this period of my life. I didn't seem to care. The peer pressure and the accent on the social ladder were even stronger at this time in my life. In my high school years I don't remember being approached by a counselor or teacher in any way to try to discuss my attending college. I realize now that I never asked to be helped in that area either. My self-esteem was very low at that point of my life. Now I believe the traumatic experience of my earlier years probably had a great deal to do with this. I was very nervous and felt guilty and afraid most of the time. I really never believed that a person like me could go to college. I believed that college was for the popular crowd. Even when colleges started sending brochures to me, it didn't occur to me that they really meant for me to apply. I just thought they didn't know who they were sending them to. They didn't really want me to to go to their college. I was poor and not real smart. Colleges were for rich, smart kids. Weren't they? That's what I thought.

Well, it seems that it didn't matter anyway. In my junior year, I fell in love and quit school to get married. I also had two children during my second decade of life. The birth of my second child brought me up to my third decade of life.

I didn't do much to continue my education during my third decade of life. I still had it in my head that I was not college material. At one time during this period of my life, I started assistant teaching in a Sunday school class. I confided to the teacher, who was also a public school teacher, that I had always wanted to be a teacher. She responded by telling me that it was not too late. I really couldn't imagine what she meant by that.

When I was twenty-five years old, my employer offered to pay for a college credit class if I wanted to attend. I was so excited that I signed up for two classes. Unfortunately, this was not to be either. I was pregnant with my third child at that time. I was very sick and had to drop from my classes. I had a beautiful little red-haired girl, but, once again, the doors of education were slammed in my face.

Accidentally, when my daughter was six months old, I got pregnant with my last child. After my last child was born, my health seemed to deteriorate. I started having anxiety attacks. I had chest pains, headaches, and dizzy spells. I ended up at the emergency room too many times to count. So, before I was thirty, I ended up getting a hysterectomy, hoping this would straighten out my life.

I did nothing else in my third decade of life to continue my education. I just fought to keep my head above water in the emotional field.

Now we come to my present decade of life. The first year or so of this decade was very hard. I was still having emotional problems, but one thing was different. I started trying to face my problems and learn to live with them. I started going to a chiropractor who helped with the physical part of my condition. I also started dealing with the emotional tragedy that happened during my early years of life. I realized that the boys that molested me were just that, boys. They probably have emotional scars because of what they did to me. Sure, I'm human. When I see them I still get mad. I still want to confront them. But what would that accomplish? I can deal with it now. I am angrier at what the event caused in my life after it happened than the event itself. It has followed me all my life and I'm sure will continue to do so. But I have learned that I have to face my obstacles and meet my challenges head-on.

I started doing this by deciding to become a nurse. I took CNA courses at the nursing home where I was working. At the same time, I enrolled at the local college for a one-credit course that would apply toward a degree in nursing. At this point in my life, I had people encouraging me to pursue a nursing career. They had confidence in me, but best of all, I was beginning to have confidence in myself. I ranked #1 grade-wise in my CNA class and got a B in my college class. I was on cloud nine and on my way.

Because I didn't have the money, I had to wait eight months before taking more classes. I wasn't familiar with college grants and loans. For the next spring semester, I did learn of the Pell Grant, applied for it, and was able to attend college full-time. By then, I had decided if I was going to college, I might as well study to be what I had always wanted to be, a teacher. I have been striving for that goal ever since.

I placed into English 101 by the skin of my teeth. A committee of three checked an essay that I wrote. They afterward told me that I was borderline for the English preparatory class. Many times since then, I have wished they had chosen the other way for me. I had a very hard time in that class. I came out with a C and a very confused attitude in that area. I did achieve an A.A. degree and continue to work on my Elementary Education degree. I still felt very uncomfortable in my English skills along with reading comprehension. I felt that I could read well enough, but I didn't feel that I comprehended what I read. I had a very hard time picking out topic sentences or putting together transition sentences to tie things together. I decided to try to remedy this by taking the reading class. I am still weak in that area, but I feel much more confident than before. I also believe that my work shows this.

I said that the first couple of years of my fourth decade of life were hard, but the last year has been even harder in a different way. Now I need to move on to a four-year college. Not only does this take money; it takes courage. I have a family, so to continue my education the way I need to, I have to make some choices that could affect all of our lives. A few semesters ago some friends and I went to check out some colleges. We decided where we wanted to go. This choice meant traveling 180 miles per day. It meant being away from my family more. The night that we got back from visiting the college of our choice, I had one of the worst nervous attacks that I had had in a long time. Coincidence? I don't think so. This caused me to continue classes where I was for a while and to seek full-time employment. I was very fortunate; I was hired full-time with full benefits at the college I attended. Three months later my husband was taken ill. The doctors tested him for everything from lung cancer to AIDS. He was diagnosed with a heart condition and emphysema. Because he was so young, this hit us pretty hard. My school work suffered for a while, but I made everything up in a matter of weeks. We had to live off just my income for twelve months, so I believe that God was watching over us. He knew that at the time that I was planning to go away to school that this obstacle would come up. He just prepared us to meet and overcome it. My education wasn't finished; it was only slowed down some. We are much stronger because of this obstacle. It has brought us closer to each other and to God. Without God there to guide me through all my decades of life, I couldn't have made it.

Well, "taking charge of my life" is an easy statement to make but not as easy to do. To take charge of my life, I must set my goals and strive to meet them. A person's goals shouldn't be too easy, but also, they shouldn't be too hard. They must be attainable. I have reached many of my goals in education, but I have many more to attain. I no longer have to sit next to the door in my classrooms, due to a fear of an anxiety attack. But I also know that if I do have one, I can work through it.

I have faced many obstacles and challenges in my life. I have conquered many but have many more to conquer. My life is richer because of my fight to get an education. I have a lovely family. My husband is now a Christian, and I am a college student. It's possible that I may never teach, but, in a sense, I am teaching right now. I am teaching, through my work at the college, that everyone has a right to an education and that there is help for those in financial need. If I see someone that needs encouragement, I can truly give it because I've been there. No, taking charge of my life isn't easy, but it is possible.

Steven Gallego

"Taking Charge of My Life." This sounds like a simple concept, but the reality is that it is one of the most difficult charges that an individual faces throughout his life. I think that most people do not want to take responsibility for their actions; I know I certainly did not. Parents do the best they can, but only trial and error can prepare us with the tools we need to successfully survive and prosper.

Let me tell you about a friend of mine, Steven. Steven lacked self-confidence, ran around with the wrong crowd, eventually used drugs, was homeless and married and divorced, all by the ripe old age of twenty-two. Talk about challenges, let me tell you about how he set himself up for a tough road and how he overcame these obstacles to get to the first rung of the ladder of success—college.

Steven tells me that his first recollection of people and places was of a feeling of inadequacy and inferiority. I remember that as a child he was terribly shy. Steven's parents once told me that he and his sister communicated in their own language. His parents were finally forced to separate the children so that Steven would have to learn to speak and communicate for himself. Steven spoke when spoken to, but he was really content to just be there. Looking back, I am certain he was afraid that he would say something stupid and embarrass himself, maybe make a mistake. Lack of confidence held him back from expressing his true feelings and from being able to really enjoy the experience of life.

Steven got by, but the inability to feel comfortable with himself led him to seek out other insecure individuals. Associating with others who had the same character flaws was like looking into a mirror and allowed him to feel safe. Steven's friends were looking for the same comfortable zone: exist, stay out of the way, never draw attention to yourself, never push yourself to exceed your expectations, because if you do, you might fail. Failure was what each of these individuals feared most and what kept them together. Steven's lack of self-esteem and confidence led him to get involved with the wrong crowd. It seems that it was a natural progression for him to seek out others sliding through life rather than those who were participating, sticking their necks out and pushing themselves. These misfits used each other to bolster their self-esteem, and certainly they would never take a chance alone or accept responsibility for their actions. Group decisions were much safer because no one individual would have to take the blame.

This selection of friends led to bigger and better things. Steven attended school, but he did not learn much. He failed to learn anything of real importance from about the sixth grade through high school. From the beginning of this year, he was falling down the ladder of life instead of climbing up the ladder. You see, in fifth grade, Steven was introduced to smoking marijuana. This indulgence stole his desire to learn. During this time period, he entered L.D. (learning disability) classes and now confesses that he was quite ashamed of himself and others in the class. Throughout high school, Steven found himself drifting into more and more L.D. classes and had no real desire or enthusiasm to improve himself. Pot smoking had become the most important part of Steven's life.

This preoccupation with drugs, however, did not stop with smoking marijuana; it progressed to hash and LSD, and concluded with an introduction to crystal methamphetamine. During this point in his life, Steven was living on the edge. He was lost and totally alienated from his family and friends, but because of the drugs could not see that problem lay with him, not them. He no longer functioned in a normal family setting because he slept all day and ran all night. His behavior became intolerable to the other members of his family. His mother was at her wit's end.

Steven partied and played until his mother forced him to make a decision. The choice was whether to become a participant in the family and life by finding a job and becoming a productive member of society, or to continue staying out all night indulging in drugs. If he chose to work and participate, then he would continue to live at home; if he wanted to continue with the drug scene, he would have to find another place to live. Steven's choice, influenced by the drugs and his peers, was drugs and the nightlife. This decision brought him a year of living on the streets. Sometimes he slept outside, sometimes in his car, or occasionally with acquaintances. Once in a while he let his folks know that he was still alive. This lifestyle was lonely, dangerous, and frightening.

After more than a year of wondering where he would sleep or

where his next meal would come from, Steven decided to go home and get straight. He tried living with his mother and her new husband, but there was too much conflict, so he moved in with his maternal grandparents. Steven stayed with them for a year, and for the first time in his life worked a full-time job and stayed away from the drugs. This year was the first time since Steven was ten years old that he had been free of drugs. During this first awakening, Steven felt that something was missing in his life. He was, after all, 20 years old, and many of his friends were married and had families.

Steven was lonely and vulnerable. He could no longer associate with his drug friends, and he hadn't formed any other relationships. It was then that he met his soon-to-be ex-wife at a friend's house. After only two weeks, he was convinced that he was in love with her. It was the first time, in a long time, that someone treated him so nicely, and he believed that she loved him as well. In about a month, Steven found himself renting an apartment for them. In addition to taking on the responsibility of caring for himself for the first time in his life, he was taking on not only his girlfriend but her seven-month-old daughter. It wasn't long before reality set in and many difficulties followed: rent, electricity, food, auto insurance and oh yes, diapers and formula for a baby. Steven's job at the airport paid enough for a single person to live on, but it certainly did not include enough money for two extra people. It was simply insufficient to meet their needs.

Life soon became a never-ending battle because there was just not enough money, and they began to bicker and fight constantly. Steven was not prepared for the responsibility of what getting out on your own meant. Oh yes, his parents had told him about all of the bills that would have to be paid and other unexpected emergencies. He, like so many inexperienced people, didn't believe that older people know what they are talking about because it won't happen to them and they'll be able to manage. You see, Steven had always lived at home and had no prior experience paying bills. His wife had never supported herself, and they felt that she should stay home with the baby. It was a grandiose idea, but far from reality when it now takes two incomes to have even a modest lifestyle.

Needless to say, the marriage didn't last long because they were both immature, inexperienced in life and love, and really had no idea what they wanted. They separated in less than a year; each was heartbroken and confused. Steven still cares for her and often thinks about the little baby girl whom he loves so deeply. It is very difficult for him because he still has not quite gotten over the fact that they are no longer together.

Steven has come to the realization that he is no longer willing to be a spectator of life. These challenges and obstacles he has overcome with the help of a loving and supportive family aided Steven to find the confidence and self-esteem he so desperately lacked. This new confidence allowed Steven to dare to dream. He decided that it was time he took charge of his life, set a goal and planned for a future. The future is a career in law enforcement, and it begins by attending college. After completing one semester, Steven is looking forward to finding a full-time job and getting back out on his own again. Steven is looking at a bright future and forward to the day he receives his college diploma, a first for himself and his family.

Carrie Graham

When I was a sophomore in high school, my mother told me that if I was planning on going to college, that I should try to find a part-time job after school. So, on my sixteenth birthday, I went down to the local supermarket and applied for a job as a cashier. It was hard in the beginning, but I knew I had to stick with it if I wanted to go to college someday. At the time I wasn't sure if I wanted to go to college or not, but if I decided to go, I thought I would at least have a little money saved. By the end of my sophomore year, I told my parents that I still did not know if I wanted to go to college. There were two reasons why I was still not sure.

The first reason I did not go directly to college after high school was I had not saved enough money. I would have had enough money if I had not bought a car. My parents told me that a car was a big responsibility, but I did not listen. (I found out very quickly how right they were.) With having to pay for insurance and also the upkeep on the car, all the money I saved was gone. At the time I thought buying a car was more important than getting a good education.

Graduation was coming fast, and I still had not saved enough money to go to college. I decided to go to the guidance office to see about applying for financial aid. They gave me some papers to bring home for my mother and me to fill in information concerning our income. I kept thinking to myself, "Maybe I will be able to go to college after all." I went home and talked it over with my mother. My mother told me that I was working, so they should not have to know what her yearly income was. There was no way to change my mother's mind, so I just decided to drop the subject. The following day I went back to the guidance office and explained to my counselor what my mother said. He told me to try to get a student loan, but when I called the people at the bank, they told me in order to apply for a student loan, I would have to have applied for financial aid. So once again I did not know what I should do. I would have applied for some scholarships, but I did not think I was smart enough to get any. I looked at some of the requirements, and most of them said you have to have a 2.5 grade point average and be in the top 20 percent of your class, and I wasn't. I told my mother that I was going to have to hold off at least a year before going to college.

There I was two years later, still not in school, because I still had not been able to save enough money. I decided to ask my parents if I could borrow money so I could take at least one class. It was very hard for me to ask because my mom is only working part-time and my step-father's construction business does not operate during the winter. They did tell me they would help, and they asked me why I did not ask them sooner. They understood that now I have not only a car to pay for but also rent and bills at the end of the month. My parents' decision to help me pay for school made me realize how much I wanted to go to school.

After deciding that I did want to go to college, I still had another problem to overcome. That was that I was afraid of failing. I did not want to go through college and always feel like a failure as I did in high school. I decided that I should give it a chance, so I reapplied to the Mount Wachusett Community College. Everything was going fine until they sent me a letter about taking the computerized placement test. I knew I had a problem with reading, but I did not want to admit it. After taking the test, I was told I had to take a fundamental reading class. I did not know if I wanted to waste money taking a class that I did not think was going to do any good.

All through grammar school and high school, I was placed in a reading lab class. I do not feel the class did anything to help me. The only thing it did was make me feel very stupid, especially in my junior and senior years in high school. I was placed in the class with seventh and eighth graders. I was very humiliated by this. It was embarrassing to me when they did better on something than I did. At the end of my senior year, they told me that I just was not trying hard enough. They said I should have scored a lot better on the test they give at the end of class. After they said this, I just felt like a failure. I knew I was doing my best, but that was not good enough for them. More pressure was added when I was told I wasn't going to graduate if I did not get an A on my English final exam. All we ever did in this English class was read a book and then have a test on the content. After my English teacher told me I might not graduate, I went home and told my mother I would rather quit than not graduate with my class. She told me to give it my all on the test. I did do my best. I read the book four times in about five weeks. Doing all of this only got me a C on the book test and a D for the semester. Again they told me I did not try. I was lucky the teacher decided to pass me so that I would graduate with my class. Even though I did pass, I didn't think I was ready for college. I knew it would be a lot tougher in college, and I did not want to set myself up for a failing grade.

I did decide to give the reading class a try. I just kept telling myself that I was going to do fine, and if I didn't I would just take the class again and again until I did pass. I only took this reading class so that I could give it my all. I was told that in college it is very hard for a teacher to work one on one with any one student. I was very thankful to get the teacher I did because she has been very good about helping me whenever I had a problem. I have been doing well on the work assigned in class, and I feel confident that I will pass this class. I am glad I gave this class a try. We took the placement test the other day. I think I did well on it. I still do not have a lot of confidence in myself when it comes to reading, but if I continue to try my hardest, I think eventually I will.

Next semester I am only taking one class because I am not yet financially able to afford any more than that. I'm beginning to realize that I'm not stupid, but that reading is just hard for me.

I think in the future it will be harder. Not only with the school work, but with working two jobs, I really don't have any free time. I have to work two jobs in order to pay bills and stay in school. At least now I feel like I'm getting somewhere. I really do not know what I want to do with my life yet, but just being in school makes me feel good about myself.

Renardo Bostick

_____

From the time I was in the ninth grade, I have dreamed of going to college, maybe not for all the right reasons, but I really wanted to go. I had my future all planned out, so I thought. I was an outstanding football player and figured to get an athletic scholarship. The football part came easy, but the academics were difficult.

My mother and teachers always warned me to keep my grades up, but my only concerns were playing football and having fun with my friends. Coming into high school in the tenth grade, my football coach encouraged me to get serious about my class work. Coach would always state that when scouts from colleges come looking for players, they would also be looking for grades. Being a young, hard-headed sophomore, I disregarded all of the warnings given to me about my grades. I had met new people and friends, and my passion for girls went wild. The years ahead looked very bright in my young eyes.

Coming into my junior year, I had to go to summer school. I had failed Algebra I. I could have still been promoted to the next grade with that failure, but I would have been ineligible to play football in my junior year. Neither my coaches nor I wanted me to miss my junior year because I had become an important part of the team, and they could not afford to lose me. I had to scrape up one hundred dollars for enrollment in summer school. My mother became so angry at me that tears came to her eyes. Seeing my mother cry like that made me feel kind of guilty and low. After seeing her so hurt, I made a promise that I would make her proud of me in some way. I figured by making good grades in the class, she would be proud of me and would redeem myself in her eyes. I made an excellent grade in the class and made my mother happy, but I could still sense that she was disappointed in me for going to summer school in the first place.

My junior year had rolled around. We had a disappointing season in football, going 3-7 for the year. The losing season was due to the loss of our star quarterback and one of my best friends, Rickey Pratcher.

Rickey and I grew up together. We attended the same schools since junior high. We always would play around about being big college football stars and someday going pro. On October 31, 1991, Rickey was shot and killed by a man desperate for drug money. When he died, it was hard on me and my friends. I could not concentrate on my class work or football. I would often find myself in class daydreaming about Rickey and the good times we had together. My mother saw the change in my behavior and knew his death affected me a lot. We had a talk one day. My mother told me that bad things are going to happen throughout my life, and all I could do was tough them out and go on with my life. She also told me to look at the mistakes Rickey and other friends made and learn from them.

At the end of the year another obstacle had to be hurdled. It was time for all juniors to take the A.C.T. This was the test my teachers prepared me for, and my coach had always preached about scoring a nineteen on the A.C.T. because scoring a nineteen was the only way incoming freshmen could be eligible for any extracurricular activities in college. When it came time for me to take the test, I was confident I could score well. The night before my test date, my mother had to leave town on a business trip. She told me to stay home and get plenty of rest. When she got off the phone, some of my friends called, asking me to go with them to a party. I figured I could go to the party, stay for a while, leave around one o'clock and have enough rest for the eight o'clock appointment. I ended up leaving the party around three o'clock in the morning. When I took the test, I was so tired I slept through half of the test. When I received my score, I was not surprised to see a bad score of a thirteen.

The summer before my senior year was a prosperous time. I was part of a school sponsored program called S.C.U.P. (School College University Program). The members of this program were seniors in high schools around Memphis who were on their way to college. It was prosperous because it helped the students with important decisions and paid us good money at the same time. The program gave students a chance to visit colleges around Tennessee and see how college life is lived.

Finally it had arrived: the year I had long waited on, the year that would decide my future in college. I promised myself I would start my senior year off strong. "Strong" meant concentrating on things such as my school work, my participation in school activities, and, of course, my football.

Things did not go as well as I had planned. Because of all the activities I was involved in, my grades stayed below average. In the first game of the year I was injured, so my performance was not impressive to college scouts. Since my grades and football performance were both poor, I had to depend heavily on my A.C.T. score. I made certain to enroll myself in the A.C.T. study sessions being held at my school. Since it was imperative that I make a nineteen and I had taken study classes, I went into the test center confident in myself. When I finally received my scores, the outcome was an eighteen, one point short of what I needed. I figured one would not make all that much of a difference and maybe the schools would make an exception for me. I sent my scores to Tennessee State University, Alcorn State, and Memphis State University. Because my grades were low and I did not meet the admission requirements of a nineteen on the A.C.T., I was denied admission into any of those colleges. I began to think there were no chances of me going to college. My coach called and brought up Knoxville College. I was not thrilled, but it was the only chance I had of going to college.

I'm now enrolled at Knoxville College. To build my grade point average up, I had to give up football. It is hard not playing for a year but worth it to help my grades. At the end of my first semester my G.P.A. was 3.2. My mother is having problems paying the tuition, and that worries me sometimes. She tells me not to worry. She says all I have to do is keep my grades up, and she will take care of the bill. Through all the obstacles, my mother has always been there for me. When I get exhausted with all of the studying and work that makes me want to quit, I just think of my mother and how hard she is working for me.

Carmen Stephens

The day I arrived at the Miami airport, I thought I was prepared for this country, which would be my new home. I was 17 years old and the new bride of a Texas oil field worker. Long before I ever dreamed that I would someday come to the United States, I had read everything I could get my hands on about North America. I took English in high school, taught by a British teacher. At that time my English vocabulary was about one hundred words. I could make sentences such as "Good morning, Mrs. Smith," "The window is open," and count endlessly.

I didn't know then that it would cost me many productive years before I understood that to live in America, one must learn to speak, read, and write English; otherwise, you are considered illiterate in the workplace. For many years I was riding the brakes of personal development, not only for myself, but for my children as well. When they were young, they were inclined to confuse Spanish and English as the same language, so they spoke a mixture of both.

Very soon after my arrival from Chile, I realized that not one person understood anything that I said. First, the pronunciation was wrong. I didn't know at the time that British English and American English have different sounds. The other reason was that I was not very fluent in either one. Also, since I do have a slight speech impairment caused by the loss of hearing in one ear due to a chronic ear infection, I do not always hear things the way people with two good ears do.

After leaving Miami, my husband took me on a tour of the Western states, where I met all his relatives. I did enjoy the traveling, but not the arrival. We were always met by those nice smiling people, looking at me and treating me almost like I was a doll. No conversation was directed to me; I could not say a single word that they understood, nor did I understand them. I was totally dependent on my husband, even to ask for a drink of water. My husband spoke several languages, including mine, so we had no trouble communicating. This was good and bad for me. Since we had no trouble talking, it took away part of the incentive to learn English.

Some years back I read a fable about five blind men who were asked to describe an elephant. Each one was led to a different part of the beast, so each one had his own idea of what it looked like. This is about the way it was with me and the United States. Each new place we went was a new experience, or a new part of the beast for me to describe to my family back in Chile.

After a few weeks of vacationing in the southwest part of the U.S., it was time to go back to work. My husband called his company and was told to go to South Dakota. This was where we settled down to housekeeping for a few months. I was pregnant with twins. It was two weeks before Christmas when we arrived in Rapid City. I thought, "This has to be the elephant's tail." The land was beautiful, at least the part I could see from my window. It was frigid cold that time of the year. My home town of Chillan seemed so far away; it was summertime there. I was cold from the inside out. This was the coldest and loneliest I had ever felt. The day before Christmas, my husband came home early, and we went shopping. It was a beautiful sunny day. I noticed that every time we went out of one store into another, the clock on the front of the Rapid City National Bank would say it was a half hour later, and the thermometer would say two degrees colder. The temperature was dropping as fast as the sun was going down. Soon the streets were covered with ice, making me slide as I walked. I didn't know why they called Rapid City "the banana belt" until the next winter, which was spent in Choteau, Montana. There I learned the definition of deep-freeze.

This was the pattern that my life took; we moved at least twice each year, winters in the cold country, summers in the hot country, always to a different town. I got to know many places and to meet many people. Somehow I managed to speak enough English and use enough body language to get by and make friends. I got to know America, to respect it, and gradually fall in love with it.

Meanwhile I read English books in my free time. Reading had been my passion since I was a child. This was my only source of intellectual growth. Since we moved so often, I could not keep many of the books I read. I did keep and treasure *War and Peace*, *Dr. Zhivago*, and a poetry book with some of the works from Gabriela Mistral and Pablo Neruda that I had brought from Chile. Everything else needed to be left behind. The family was growing, and more things were necessary to take along. I learned from the wives of my husbands' fellow workers.

They taught me to drive a car, to cook American food, and to sew. I made all the children's clothes and even baked pies. Although my pies were like "jaw breakers," since I didn't use any shortening in the crust, my kids thought they were the greatest pies. (I still feel that shortening is unnecessary in this type of food preparation.) I adopted many things from America, but some I customized to my beliefs.

The English language always seemed to elude me. As hard as I tried, I could never get things right. In our sixth year in the United States, we were transferred to Houston, Texas. That was the first big city we were in for any length of time. There we enrolled the twins in preschool, and I enrolled in an English class at the city college. I was very eager to get to school; all my past desire for learning was creeping inside at once. In this school I made friends with a girl from Venezuela named Alicia. Alicia was familiar with Houston, so we visited many factory outlets together. One day I accompanied her to get a haircut at a place where it was "muy economico"; it turned out that it was a cosmetology school. I was very impressed to find that some of the girls in the school did not speak English, and they were there learning a career. I didn't waste any time. I took all the information pertaining to enrollment home to my husband, and after convincing him, I enrolled in cosmetology school. The manager was very nice; she made an exception to allow me to take my son to class, just like the teacher in my English class. I believe if Alicia had needed teeth extracted that day instead of a hair cut, I would have tried to enter Dental School.

The next Monday after the English class, I started this new school. I got my little boy equipped with a lunch box, a Lego set and a Tonka truck for him to play with. I don't know if the long hours my son spent playing with these toys on the floor of the cosmetology school had any influence on his chosen career, but today Jimmy is a geotechnical engineer.

My husband was still traveling, but he was going alone now to give me time to finish school. Right after the girls were out of school, we needed to move to Waynesboro, Mississippi. It would have been too much of a strain on the family for me to stay in Houston. I had finished the English semester a week before, but not the cosmetology course. To recoup some of the hours I had put into the beauty school, I got a manicurist's license. But the additional hours were lost. Once again we moved; it was sad to leave behind the school and my friends. It seemed that all my efforts were for nothing. In reality I was wrong in thinking that I had wasted my time while I lived in Houston. Besides being able to take care of my family's hair needs, the period of English classes I took, along with the communication and socializing I was doing in the beauty school, did improve my understanding of English, I didn't realize at the time that I was also learning to read lips in English. I was beginning to be the second little man touching the elephant, this time at the leg.

After settling in Waynesboro, we heard that there was a good otolaryngologist in Jackson named Dr. Snyder. I had been to many doctors with my ear, in the hopes of finding one that could do something for the infection and maybe give me back some of my hearing. After the first visit with Dr. Snyder, somehow I knew that this doctor was different. I started going to him once a week for treatment. Dr. Snyder tried many different medications and approaches until he finally did accomplish what no other doctor had been able to; he healed my ear infection. Some months after stopping the treatments, he gave me a hearing test. The results were I had lost almost all the hearing from my left ear, and some from my right. He told me a hearing aid would not be of any help at this time. That is part of the reason why English was so hard for me to learn.

After a year in Waynesboro we were transferred to Rio de Janeiro, Brazil. We were in many countries around the world for the next twenty years. We would come to the U.S. for a vacation every year or two, for a month, sometimes two. I attended various colleges in different countries, taking classes in bilingual secretarial work, medical assistance, home economics, and international relations. My goal was to work for an international organization.

My English didn't improve much during this time. I kept up with the English and Spanish reading, now adding Portuguese. In this period, I was like the third blind man, stroking the ivory tusk of the elephant. It feels smooth, strong, sturdy, highly polished; at the end it was smooth, rounded, not sharp. Life was good to us as emissaries of the U.S. That was our golden era, a long time ago. But like everyone, we got older. We came back to Houston, and then my husband had a heart attack, and later, bypass surgery.

Today I am faced with the necessity to work. Again, the lack of English skills has put limitations on what I am able to do. I have managed to work in agencies where I need Spanish, but I have stumbled from one job to another for the last few years. I know I cannot get any further without greater command of the English language.

My time has come; I have made the decision to really learn English. I have just finished my first semester in college, and I received good grades. That is not the only reason that I feel good. I feel that I belong here now, that I am growing.

Still many interpretations can be given to the elephant, as a blind person might see it in his mind if we follow the tale, but, for myself, I no longer look at one little area of anything. The day I enrolled in college, I took the bandage off my eyes. It took me a long time to realize, from the day I arrived in Miami, with a suitcase full of hopes, until today, that complete command of the English language is the vessel that will take me to wherever I want to go.

List of Winners

First Place Essay
Ricki Gutierrez, *Oklahoma City Community College*

Second Place Essays
Kimberly S. Baird, *Muskegon Community College*
Vickie Jean Burress, *Indiana Vocational Technical College*
Christina J. Jones, *Arkansas State University*
Bettie Jo Mellott, *Ohio University*
Elda Sara Morgan, *Corning Community College*

Third Place Essays

Grant Berry, *Muskegon C College*
Michael Anthony Couch, *Indiana University at Kokomo*
Stacy Ebeling, *Sheridan College*
Joy Lynn Fox, *Pellissippi State Tech. C College*
Greg Francis, *Indiana University at Kokomo*
Leatrice Muniz, *Hudson County C College*
Regina Lynn Rayder, *Roane State C College*

Ruby Rolon, *Roane State C College*
Regina Ruiz, *Burlington County College*
Rose Ann Snell, *Glendale C College*
Raynard C. Sousis, *Austin Peay State University*
Carolyn Ann Street, *Central Arizona College*
Mary K. Vant, *Prince George's C College*
Kevin Shawn Watkins, *Tarrant Cty. Jr. College*
Lacey Wray, *D'Youville College*

Honorable Mention

Juan Angel, *Blue Mountain C College*
Fred Balmer*, *Lamar University at Orange*
Lisa Barnett, *Kilgore College*
Jama Bile, *Central Arizona College*
Aquila Bishop, *Central Arizona College*
Lydia Blair, *Pellissippi State Tech. C College*
Renardo Bostick, *Knoxville College*
Trena F. Brown, *South Suburban College*
Sharon Conlin*, *Holyoke C College*
Carol Copsey, *Atlantic C College*
Ronald R. D'Avignon, *Pellissippi State Tech. C College*
Gwendolyn Davis, *Pierce College*
Andrew Drahos, *Utica College*
LeQuita Foster, *Arkansas State University*
Steven Gallego, *Phoenix College*
Donna Garriott, *Middle Tenn. State University*
Carrie Graham, *Mt. Wachusett C College*
Kathy Haltiwanger, *Tri-County Tech. College*
Christopher D. Hanson, *Tarrant Cty. Jr. College*
Dave J. Hanson, *Essex County College*
Sherry Johnston, *Phoenix College*
Lynda S. Kissior, *Roane State C College*
Marilyn Kent-Krigger, *North Lake College*
Edward P. Kruger, *Erie C College*
William Leos, Jr., *Phoenix College*

Lavern Little, *Kilgore College*
Xinrong Liu, *Iowa Western C College*
Lynn Macklin*, *Holyoke C College*
Irina Marjan*, *C College of Philadelphia*
Catherine R. Mott, *College of Great Falls*
Josephine T. Nguyen, *Middlesex County College*
Ruth Norris, *Arkansas State University*
Angie S. Osborne, *Virginia Highlands C College*
Paulina Pen, *Holyoke C College*
Bernadete Piassa, *Bucks County C College*
Jay Puterbaugh, *Indiana University at Kokomo*
George Nagba-Gayou Roberts, Jr., *College of Mt. Saint Vincent*
Awa Fanta Sagnia, *Muskegon C College*
Leo Solvick*, *Muskegon C College*
Carmen Stephens, *Kings River C College*
Isaac W. Thaler, *Broward C College*
Patrick Tyrell, *Knoxville College*
Becky Vanderputte, *Muskegon C College*
Sandy Wagner, *Clarion University of Penna.*
Terri L. Waring, *Bronx C College*
Stevan Weise, *Mississippi Gulf Coast C College*
Anita Werry, *Shepherd College*
Michelle Elaine Wilson, *Sinclair C College*
Lyndy Worsham, *Lane C College*
Margaret J. Younger, *C College of Aurora*

Where noted with an asterisk, the author's name has been changed for personal reasons.